THE POLICE TRAFFIC CONTROL FUNCTION

ABOUT THE AUTHOR

Paul B. Weston had a progressively successful career in the New York City Police Department on a "fast track" promotion examination system pioneered by New York's feisty Mayor Fiorello H. LaGuardia and his Municipal Civil Service Commission. When a new list of successful applicants for police officer was published, the Mayor hired the top two hundred, then the commission set the date for the next sergeant's examination to allow this group just enough seniority to qualify for the test. In turn, the top group of sergeants became eligible for the lieutenant's test, and likewise the captain's examination. It was a tough program as seniority could earn up to twenty points on the possible score of 200 and the "fast track" candidates had less than one full point of seniority!

Weston placed on the top of each list and became a captain in twelve years and two months—far ahead of the more common 18 to 20 years. From this jump start, he moved through the appointed ranks (no tests) of Deputy Inspector, Inspector, and Deputy Chief Inspector. The last two promotions were made by Police Commissioner Stephen P. Kennedy for good work in the Traffic Division.

After retirement from the N.Y.C.P.D., Weston joined the "police science" faculty at California State College, Sacramento, worked through all the changes of the police unit to a Division of Criminal Justice, the college to a university, and Paul to retirement and Professor Emeritus status.

Professor Weston now lives in the Sacramento area with his daughter and granddaughter.

THE POLICE TRAFFIC CONTROL FUNCTION

Fifth Edition

By

PAUL B. WESTON

Deputy Chief Inspector (Ret.)
New York City Police Department
Professor Emeritus
Division of Criminal Justice
School of Health and Human Services
California State University
Sacramento, California

CHARLES C THOMAS • PUBLISHER
Springfield • Illinois • U.S.A.

Published and Distributed Throughout the World by

CHARLES C THOMAS • PUBLISHER
2600 South First Street
Springfield, Illinois 62794-9265

© *1960, 1968, 1975, 1978, and 1996 by* CHARLES C THOMAS • PUBLISHER

ISBN 0-398-06567-5 (cloth)
ISBN 0-398-06568-3 (paper)

Library of Congress Catalog Card Number: 95-25888

First Edition, 1960
Second Edition, First Printing, 1968
Second Edition, Second Printing, 1969
Second Edition, Third Printing, 1970
Second Edition, Fourth Printing, 1971
Third Edition, 1974
Third Edition, Second Printing, 1977
Fourth Edition, 1978
Fifth Edition, 1996

With THOMAS BOOKS *careful attention is given to all details of manufacturing
and design. It is the Publisher's desire to present books that are satisfactory as to
their physical qualities and artistic possibilities and appropriate for their particular
use.* THOMAS BOOKS *will be true to those laws of quality that assure a good
name and good will.*

Printed in the United States of America

Library of Congress Cataloging-in-Publication Data

Weston, Paul B.
    The police traffic control function / by Paul B. Weston. — 5th
ed.
        p.   cm.
    Includes bibliographical references and index.
    ISBN 0-398-06567-5. — ISBN 0-398-06568-3 (paper)
    1. Traffic police.   2. Traffic regulations.   3. Traffic accident
investigation.   I. Title.
HV8079.5.W47   1996
363.2'332 — dc20   95-258888
                                                                    CIP

Dedicated to William B. Melnicoe (1926–1987), professor and chairman, Division of Criminal Justice, School of Health and Human Services, California State University, Sacramento. "Bill" was a nationally recognized expert in traffic accident reconstruction, and a qualified expert witness in the courts of six states. We taught together for twenty-five years.

PREFACE

This is an extensive revision of a good book. Material from the Fourth Edition (1978) was reviewed and updated. About 20 percent was deleted, the remainder was rewritten or merged with new ideas and practices. One "new" chapter is a joinder of two of the Fourth Edition chapters. This new edition has three new chapters: (a) Street and Highway Safety—establishes a "system" for traffic safety; (b) Zero Tolerance—Driving Under Influence—hardball enforcement aimed at drinking drivers; and (c) Speed Management—slowing down speeding drivers.

The focus of this text is still on the police role in accident reduction and selective enforcement. However, there is a strong secondary focus on new ideas and innovations likely to be successful in getting drinking drivers off our streets and highways, and new procedures to confront the reality of highway, convenience, and the ideal mph for all drivers.

The new sixteen-chapter development is structured as an expanded course description for a one-semester course in police traffic control in community colleges, or four-year colleges and universities. Marginal headings throughout each chapter promote reader comprehension, and could be useful in preparing lesson plans. Also helpful to readers and students are the newly enlarged graphics (charts and diagrams), a new Glossary defining words and phrases of traffic safety or not in common use, and the index.

The Fifth Edition is a better book.

PAUL B. WESTON

CONTENTS

THE POLICE TRAFFIC CONTROL FUNCTION

Chapter 1

STREET AND HIGHWAY SAFETY

Police traffic control is a focused attempt by local and state police to lessen the homicide and mayhem caused by traffic accidents.

State police, deputy sheriffs, and city police monitor moving traffic and enforce reasonable rules for safe driving enacted by state legislatures, and promptly investigate traffic accidents to determine when, where, who, what, how, and why circumstances. In this joinder of activity, police managers can gain a basic understanding of the factors involved in past accidents and guide their monitoring activity toward multiaccident locations or unsafe driving practices found to be contributors to such accidents, or both.

The ultimate goal of police traffic control is to enhance the safe movement of people and cargo on a street and highway system, and to reduce the incidence of traffic accidents through a basic understanding of the factors involved.

Agents of law enforcement agencies "working traffic" confront a problem of frightening dimensions:

1. Millions of vehicles and licensed drivers
2. Miles of streets and highways
3. Billions of vehicle miles of travel each year
4. Over 42,000 fatal traffic accidents annually
5. A mileage death rate (number of deaths per 100 million vehicle miles of travel) of almost two persons per 100 million vehicle miles of travel.*

Traffic Safety System

There is a great need for a systematic arrangement of the major elements of street and highway safety which will encourage user-friendly channels of communication and cooperation. In past years, automotive

---

*Statistics on traffic accidents are reported monthly by the National Safety Council in *Traffic Safety*.

and highway engineers hardly ever queried police or emergency medical personnel as to how vehicles and highways were unsafe; nor did legislators or motor vehicle administration executives seek much help from the here-and-now agencies of police and paramedics as to modifying laws and licensing to enhance driver safety.

The driver would be at the center of this system, not as scapegoat but rather as a focal point for to-and-fro information on driver experience and measures planned to improve driver safety. This is not a return to the "nut behind the wheel" belief, but a timely recognition of the fact that drivers and their passengers are the end-products of traffic safety measures.

The major elements of this traffic safety system, in addition to the police, are:

1. Vehicle manufacturers and their engineers and designers
2. State legislators and, sometimes, local lawmakers
3. Department of Motor Vehicles (DMV)
4. Highway and traffic engineers
5. Driver
6. Emergency Medical Services (EMS) (see Fig. 1).

The two major influences on the traffic safety system are the number of traffic accidents and current public opinion. This is a newsworthy area. Are fatalities in traffic accidents increasing? Is the year-end total of all accidents higher than the past year? Has the locality experienced a multivehicle accident recently—20 or more vehicles involved? Public opinion responds to such events.

Automakers/Engineers/Designers

Automakers must build occupant-safe cars and trucks. The giant corporations that make cars and trucks seek to set their own pace in providing vehicle safety improvements. Executives and public relations personnel of these manufacturers uniformly claim the need to be competitive and cite cost as the most valuable factor in selling their products, and that the costs of new safety features must be borne by car and truck buyers.

For years, airbags were sold only as a high-priced option. Prompt public demand resulted in driver and front-passenger seat airbags becoming standard equipment in many cars.

Drivers are often forced to make stops to avoid a collision, but with

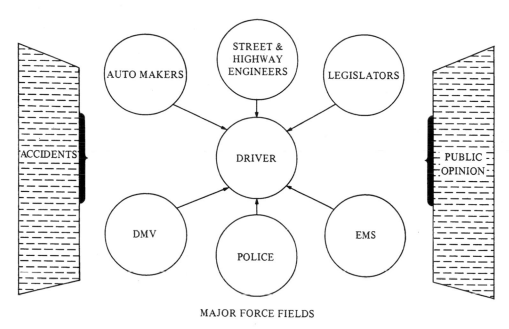

MAJOR FORCE FIELDS

Figure 1. The traffic system: six units focusing on the driver, and responsive to public opinion and the monthly/yearly accident rate.

standard-issue brakes experience skidding and loss of control—and do not avoid damaging impacts. Antilock braking systems remedy this failure of a major mechanical feature of a vehicle. Unfortunately, it is being routed to consumers along the same route as airbags· option to standard equipment.

The recall of many vehicles by automakers and successful lawsuits against them for faulty design (leading to fatal and serious accidents) indicate the potential of vehicle defects to cause or contribute to traffic accidents.*

Hopefully, automakers will soon conclude innovative safety modifications in their cars and trucks are "good business." Vehicles flaming out because of poorly-situated gasoline tanks, rolling over due to design instability, and folding up or tearing apart because of poor-to-lousy crashworthiness are certainly "bad business"! These defects aggravate the seriousness of accidents.

Automakers may be reluctant to participate in developing the necessary relationships for meaningful linkage with others with a common

---

*Ralph Nader, *Unsafe At Any Speed* (New York, Pocket Books, 1966), p. 33.

interest in upgrading safety on streets and highways. However, each manufacturer is an important agency-in-place. They make the cars and trucks in daily use.

Legislators

In a democratic system of law making, the interests of legislators are in harmony with the value judgments and general interests of a community. Popular will reflects a general public opinion at the time a new law or an amendment to an enacted law is proposed. Legislators commonly are guided by this public opinion, but can be influenced by special interest groups.

Once a law is enacted it begins to live a life of its own, independent of the circumstances of its enactment. It is generally in harmony with legislative intent at the time of original enactment, but its growth or diminishment is influenced by the ebb and flow of public opinion.

Lawmakers are responsive to automobile associations, Mothers Against Drunk Driving (MADD), and like organizations. Police and other elements of a traffic safety system are likely to find these men and women eager to support two-way communication likely to promote common interests.

Department of Motor Vehicles (DMV)

DMV administrators have an awesome statewide responsibility, no less than developing and supervising:

1. A comprehensive driver licensing registry
2. An extensive system for the registration of all motor vehicles
3. A uniform system for recording police traffic accident reports.

A bottom line for all drivers is to get a license. Applicants must exhibit knowledge of the state's vehicle code and display reasonable driving skills. Full requirements vary from state to state.

Another basic fact of life for all licensed drivers is to keep their license. Reckless and dangerous driving and being involved in an unusual number of accidents threatens the possession of a driver's license. Repeated convictions for driving while under the influence of alcohol and/or drugs are likely to result in license suspension or revocation. Chronic illness, severe emotional problems, and like disabilities may not warrant license suspension or revocation, but may justly specify restrictions.

Driver conduct behind the wheel is easily noted by DMV monitoring of the in-house accident reports, vehicle registration numbers, and police reports of drivers arrested or cited for vehicle code violations. Upgraded computer systems in most states can now furnish data on cars and drivers involved in accidents, and drivers arrested or cited for vehicle code violations, to a home-state DMV.

A state's DMV is a unit within the traffic safety system effectively monitoring the conduct of its resident driver population and taking appropriate action when warranted. In addition, a DMV can serve other units in the system by opening up new and innovative retrieval paths to stored information.

Traffic and Highway Engineers

Traffic engineers study vehicle movement, volume, and patterns. They use signs and pavement markings, traffic signals, and changes in the direction of traffic on streets to guide, direct, and control traffic movement. They make changes in the geometric design of streets and their intersections when warranted to meaningfully improve traffic flow and/or safety. Past accidents are studied by these men and women in a traffic engineering department to discover what happened and what they can do about it.

Highway engineers develop improvements for existing highways and design new highways. Better engineered roads mean less driver error and a more forgiving environment (such as "breakaway" light standards) when accidents do occur. Well-designed highways can prevent accidents.

The Interstate Highway System has made a significant contribution to safer highways and, in turn, accident reduction. The basic system now totals thousands of miles of highway, east and west, north and south. The interstate network was planned for the safety and convenience of road users. Billions of vehicle miles of vehicle travel on this highway system and the low fatality rate indicates that these highways are safe.

There is no excuse for unsafe highways. The basic concept of a humanitarian government demands that federal, state, and local officials require no less from highway engineering staffs than *safe* highways.

Drivers

Drivers are assorted: men/women, teen/young adult, elderly/aged, chronically ill/disabled, short/tall, and flyweight/heavyweight. Baseline driving skills are known, but the skills of some drivers increase with time on the road while others degrade their skills during bouts of boredom, anger, or depression. Some drivers will wipe out most of their skills by driving under the influence of alcohol or drugs.

In any event, all drivers should be provided with an occupant-safe car or truck, a street or highway design lessening conflict with other vehicles, and police monitoring of all drivers to reduce illegal and unsafe driving.

This unit of the traffic safety system is an ongoing resource as to why drivers have accidents and the possible human error involved.

Emergency Medical Services (EMS)

A new team of trained paramedics arrive at traffic-accident scenes in the early postcrash stage of these accidents. They arrive in a fully-equipped ambulance, go right to work providing skilled medical care to injured participants, and load the severely injured victim(s) into their ambulance, and race to a designated hospital—conferring enroute with personnel of the hospital's emergency room or trauma center. Two ambulances—or more—can be dispatched, if required, and helicopters are available for transporting victims in many areas to reduce significantly the travel time to the hospital.

This is EMS in action. Past performance evaluation by both victims and police officers is usually *excellent.* Police have felt inadequate to properly care for victims in this postcrash period, and delays in ambulance arrivals were agonized frustration. Victims experiencing their help at an accident scene view them as miracle workers: humanitarians doing field work.

These here-and-now aspects of EMS indicate a close relation to the police unit of the traffic control system. This relationship indicates the likelihood of real communication and cooperation in future years.

Networking

What had once been an informal network of under-bosses in New York City to get things done or queries answered is now the route of an increasing number of formal and semiformal communications. While the chief of the police traffic division had to go through channels and deal with the director of the state DMV or the city's chief traffic engineer, his assistants could telephone a friend in the DMV or the traffic engineering office and get results in hours—not days.

This enables all men and women to openly talk to others in the traffic safety system about common interests and the how-to of getting things done—or undone.

Toppling the chief executive from the top of an organization and empowering lesser managers and their subordinates to communicate with their peers in other traffic safety agencies is new and innovative—and useful. Bringing together all the relevant parties that need to be coordinated is also considered a fine way to run a for-profit business.*

---

*Gerald Ross and Michael Kay. *Toppling the Pyramids—Redefining the Way Companies Are Run*, (New York, Times Books: Random House, 1994), pp. 40–41.

Chapter 2

TRAFFIC LAW

A state vehicle code provides for uniformity within the state for laws relating to highway use and vehicle operation. A similarity of vehicle codes from state to state would extend this concept of uniform laws to govern highway use and vehicle operation to highway users who travel from state to state. Residents of any state could be expected to know, and comply with, the provisions of a state's vehicle code; uniformity of vehicle codes from state to state would transfer this knowledge and voluntary compliance far beyond the borders of a home state of any highway user.

Most vehicle codes have been enacted despite public apathy. Legislative intent has been to enact reasonable laws based on the objective of any vehicle code: the safe movement of traffic.

The provisions of a vehicle code are sanctioned law, even though most of the regulated actions are noncriminal. However, to many working policemen this is academic; the death, destruction, and damage resulting from the unsafe and unlawful operation of vehicles is criminal in its needless and often wanton disregard for the rights—and lives—of others.

Accident reduction through police enforcement of vehicle code regulations is based upon the enforcement of the sections of the code relating to *moving violations:* unlawful behavior of the operator or illegal condition of the vehicle while the vehicle is in operation. These "movers" are generally grouped together in a vehicle code under the heading "Rules of The Road."*

---

*California Vehicle Code, Department of Motor Vehicles, Sacramento, California, 1995. Division 11, "Rules of the Road," Sections 21052–23336.

Failing to Keep to the Right

As a general rule, all vehicle codes in the United States require a vehicle to be driven upon the right half of a roadway. The exceptions to this rule are

1. When overtaking and passing another vehicle proceeding in the same direction under the rules governing such movement.
2. When placing a vehicle in a lawful position for, and when the vehicle is lawfully making, a left turn.
3. When the right half of a roadway is closed to traffic under construction or repair.
4. Upon a roadway designated and sign-posted for one-way traffic.
5. When the roadway is not of sufficient width.
6. When the vehicle is necessarily traveling so slowly as to impede the normal movement of traffic, that portion of the highway adjacent to the right edge of the roadway may be utilized temporarily when it is in a condition permitting safe operation.

Operators of vehicles are required to respect the integrity of barriers on divided highways, double parallel solid painted lines on the highway (usually white or yellow), and authorized signs temporarily designating "off-center" traffic movement. Roadways are frequently divided by pavement markings into clearly marked traffic lanes. Operators are expected to keep their vehicles within the confines of a designated lane and not move from such lane until the operator has first ascertained that such vehicle movement can be made with safety. Drivers of vehicles proceeding in opposite directions are required to pass each other to the right, either remaining in the designated traffic lanes, or upon roadways without such pavement markings, giving the approaching driver at least half of the main traveled portion of the roadway whenever possible.

Because of numerous accidents at so-called "blind" curves, many vehicle codes require operators of vehicles to give an audible warning with the horn of their vehicle upon approaching any curve where the view is obstructed within a distance of two hundred or three hundred feet along the highway. All states also forbid the use of any on-ramps or off-ramps by wrong-way drivers. California has erected attention-getting signs on such ramps and other entrances and exits: *Stop — Go Back — You Are Going the Wrong Way!*

Overtaking and Passing

The driver of an overtaking vehicle is cautioned not to follow the car ahead too closely in his initial movement of this driving maneuver. The California Vehicle Code forbids this unsafe driving practice as follows: "The driver of a motor vehicle shall not follow another vehicle more closely than is reasonable and prudent, having due regard for the speed of such vehicle and the traffic upon, and the condition of, the roadway."

Most states also write into their vehicle codes a restriction against following authorized emergency vehicles* too closely. Years ago, it was quite common to observe cars following fire engines responding to a fire alarm, and often racing them in an impromptu and hazardous speed contest. Vehicles in California, other than an authorized emergency vehicle, should not be driven closer than three hundred feet to any authorized emergency vehicle being operated in response to an emergency call, in rescue operations, in pursuit of an actual or suspected law violator, or in response to a fire alarm (or a fire department vehicle moving from place to place because of an emergency call). The driver of the authorized emergency vehicle is required to sound a siren as may be reasonably necessary, and the vehicle must display a lighted red light visible from the front as a warning to approaching vehicles.

Multilane highways have made the overtaking and passing of other vehicles a comparatively safe operation. A vehicle is not following too closely when it is being driven in a different lane than the vehicle ahead when both lanes accommodate traffic proceeding in the same direction. However, the larger percentage of roadways in any street and highway system are still secondary roads which only accommodate one lane of traffic in each direction. To overtake and pass another vehicle in these conditions requires the car to move close to the vehicle ahead and then, when safe, to pass it by utilizing the traffic lane normally reserved for opposing traffic.

In California, this complex driving maneuver is outlined for vehicle operators on two-way roads as follows:

1. *Overtaking and Passing to the Left:* The driver of a vehicle overtaking another vehicle proceeding in the same direction on a road-

---

*Usually identified as ambulances, police cars and motorcycles, fire department vehicles, and vehicles of public agencies used in responding to emergency, rescue, or lifesaving calls, or private vehicles specifically licensed as authorized emergency vehicles.

way accommodating opposing traffic shall pass to the left at a safe distance without interfering with the safe operation of the overtaken vehicle, subject to the limitation and exceptions hereinafter stated.

2. *Passing Without Sufficient Clearance:* On a two-lane highway with traffic in opposing directions, no vehicle shall be driven to the left side of the center of the roadway in overtaking and passing another vehicle proceeding in the same direction unless the left side is clearly visible and free of oncoming traffic for a sufficient distance ahead to permit such overtaking and passing to be completely made without interfering with the safe operation of any vehicle approaching from the opposite direction. In any event the overtaking vehicle shall return to the right-hand side of the roadway before coming within one hundred feet of any vehicle approaching from the opposite direction.

3. *When Driving on the Left-Hand Side is Prohibited:* No vehicle shall at any time be driven to the left side of a two-way roadway under the following conditions:
    A. When approaching the crest of a grade or upon a curve in the highway where the driver's view is obstructed within such distance as to create a hazard in the event another vehicle might approach from the opposite direction;
    B. When the view is obstructed upon approaching within one hundred feet of any bridge, viaduct, or tunnel; or
    C. When approaching within one hundred feet of or when traversing any intersection or railroad grade crossing.

4. *Passing on the Right:* The driver of a motor vehicle may overtake and pass to the right of another vehicle when conditions permit such movement in safety, but only under the following circumstances:
    A. When the vehicle overtaken is making or about to make a left turn;
    B. Upon a highway within a business or residence district with unobstructed pavement of sufficient width for two or more lines of moving vehicles in the direction of travel;
    C. Upon a highway outside a business or residence district with unobstructed pavement of sufficient width and clearly marked for two or more lines of moving traffic in the direction of travel.
    D. Upon a one-way street; or
    E. Upon a highway divided into two roadways where traffic is restricted to one direction upon each of such roadways,

and

  F. In no event shall such movement be made by driving off the paved or main-traveled portion of the roadway.

 5. ***Passing Streetcars, Trolley Coaches or Buses:*** The driver of a vehicle overtaking a multiple-passenger vehicle shall stop in the rear of such vehicles when they are stopped or about to stop, observe established safety zones by reducing speed to 10 mph and less and by exercising due caution for the safety of pedestrians, and not pass to the left of a multipassenger vehicle operating on tracks unless so directed by a police officer, on a one-way street, or when the location of the tracks prevent passing on the right.

 6. ***Passing on Grades:*** In the event any vehicle is being operated on any grade outside a business or residence district at a speed of less than 20 mph, no person operating any other motor vehicle shall attempt to overtake and pass such slow-moving vehicle unless the overtaking vehicle is operated at a speed of at least 10 mph in excess of the speed of the overtaken vehicle, nor unless the passing movement is completed within a total distance not greater than one quarter of a mile.

 7. ***Yield for Passing:*** Except when passing on the right is permitted and can be done with safety, the driver of the vehicle in front (being overtaken) shall give way to the right in favor of the overtaking vehicle on audible signal and shall not increase the speed of his vehicle until completely passed by the overtaking vehicle.

The driver of any vehicle approaching a horse-drawn vehicle, any ridden animal, or any livestock shall keep his vehicle under control, slowing or stopping when necessary or when signalled or requested to do so by any person driving, riding, or in charge of the animal or livestock. This yielding by vehicle operators safeguards the animal or livestock and insures the safety of the person driving or riding the animal or in charge of the livestock.

Turning and Stopping

All vehicle codes make some provision to guide vehicle operators in making right and left turns, specify certain stops required of motorists, and require appropriate signals which will warn other drivers of the turn or stop.

At intersections, when right- or left-hand turns are required, notice of such requirement is given by clearly marked traffic lanes and traffic-control devices or by posted signs; when such turns are prohibited at intersections, notice of such prohibition is given by posted signs. There is also a developing trend to post signs at intersections to indicate whether a U-turn is permitted or prohibited, or to indicate the lane from which U-turns may be made (when two lanes are provided for left-turn "storage" and turning).

The driver of a vehicle intending to turn is usually required to do so as follows:

1. *Right Turns:* Both the approach for a right turn and the right turn shall be made as close as practicable to the right-hand curb or edge of the roadway, except when turning from a one-way highway at an intersection where a right turn may be completed in any lane lawfully available to traffic moving in such direction upon the roadway being entered.
2. *Left Turns:* The driver of a vehicle intending to turn left shall make his approach as close as practicable to the left-hand edge of the extreme left-hand lane or portion of the roadway lawfully available to traffic moving in the direction of travel of such vehicle and, when turning at an intersection, the left turn shall not be made before entering the intersection. After entering the intersection, the left turn shall be made so as to leave the intersection in a lane lawfully available to traffic moving in such direction upon the roadway being entered.
3. *Middle-lane Turns:* On highways with three marked lanes for traffic in one direction which terminates at an intersecting highway accommodating traffic in both directions, the driver of a vehicle in the middle lane may turn right or left into any lane of traffic moving in such direction upon the roadway being entered (see Fig. 2).
4. *U-turns:* The driver of a vehicle in a business district shall not turn so as to proceed in the opposite direction except at intersections or where openings in a divided highway have been provided for such turns. In residence districts no U-turn shall be made when any other vehicle is approaching from either direction within two hundred feet, except at an intersection where the approaching traffic is controlled by an official traffic control device. U-turns

shall not be made on any highway where the driver of a vehicle making a U-turn does not have an unobstructed view for two hundred feet in both directions along the highway and of any traffic thereon. U-turns shall not be made in the driveway or other approaches to a fire station.

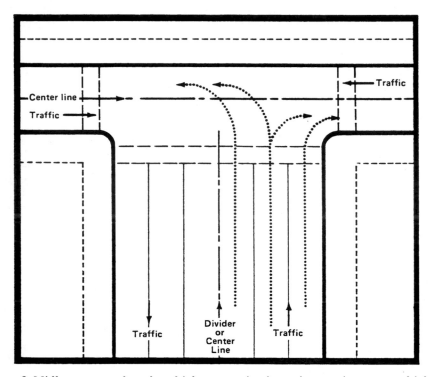

Figure 2. Midlane turns—three-lane highway terminating at intersecting two-way highway.

Special stops at railroad crossings are required of operators of multiple-passenger vehicles, tank trucks and vehicles carrying explosive substances; all motorists are required to stop at any entrance to a highway, any intersection or any railroad grade crossing signposted with a stop sign. The stop is to be made at a *limit line,* if marked on the pavement of the roadway, either before entering the crosswalk on the near side of the intersection or before entering the intersection or highway when a crosswalk is not evident (see Fig. 3).

Some intersections are signposted with stop signs *within* the intersection. In these cases, the stop is made where indicated by the sign, and limit lines are usually marked on the pavement. Stops shall also be made,

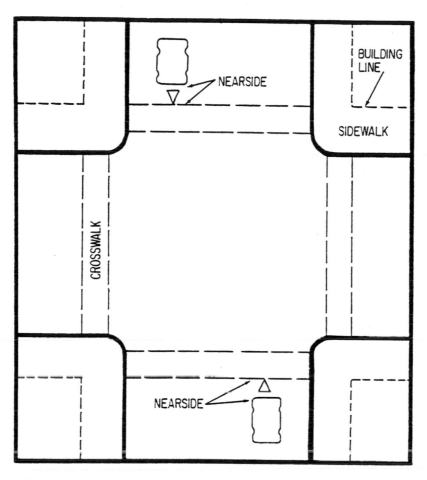

Figure 3. The intersection is bounded by crosswalks. The "near side" of a crosswalk is related to vehicles approaching intersection.

when required by traffic conditions, at intersections and entrances to roadways signposted with yield signs. Other stops are required in accordance with traffic control devices and require vehicular traffic facing the device to stop at limit lines, if marked, at crosswalks on the near side of the intersection or before entering the intersection if crosswalks are not evident.

Where to stop when one is required to do so by a traffic control device is best described as the place in the roadway where the stop will make its expected contribution to safe driving. This is also true of a motorist's duty after stopping. Legislative intent in enacting these provisions of law was to bring a vehicle to a stop in the expectation that the operator would look carefully, would judge speeds and distances of approaching cars as any "reasonable and prudent" driver,* and would proceed only when there is no hazard from oncoming vehicles.

Starting or backing a vehicle is closely related to turning and stopping a vehicle from a viewpoint of equal hazards. However, only the broad rule of "reasonable safety" governs starting or backing of vehicles: No person shall start a vehicle stopped, standing, or parked on a highway, or back a vehicle on a highway, until such movement can be made with reasonable safety.

Both turning and stopping maneuvers require advance notice of a driver's intention. California has two very concise but quite clear provisions on this need for signaling turns or stops. They are worded as follows:

1. **Required Signals for Turning Movements.** No person shall turn a vehicle from a direct course or move right or left upon a roadway until such movement can be made with reasonable safety and then only after the giving of an appropriate signal in the manner provided in this chapter in the event any other vehicle may be affected by the movement.

2. **Signal When Stopping.** No person shall stop or suddenly decrease the speed of a vehicle on a highway without first giving an appropriate signal in the manner provided in this chapter to the driver of any vehicle immediately to the rear when there is opportunity to give the signal.

Methods of signalling are now well standardized across the country, with mechanical signal devices on cars and trucks serving to warn other motorists of turns or stops. When required signals are given by hand and arm, standard procedure is that the driver give the signals from the left side of the vehicle. These standard signals are as follows:

Left turn signal: Hand and arm extended horizontally beyond the side of the vehicle.

Right turn signal: Hand and arm extended upward beyond the side of the vehicle.

---

*The "reasonable and prudent" man concept relates to care versus negligence. Ordinary care (as opposed to negligence) is the care which reasonable men exercise under ordinary circumstances. Negligence is the doing of an act which a reasonably prudent person would not do, or the failure to do something which a reasonably prudent person would do. Negligence is a relative term. The questioned behavior must be examined in relation to all of the relevant circumstances. Reasonably prudent persons react differently to different circumstances. The behavior standard is that conduct which might reasonably have been expected of a person of ordinary prudence in the same circumstances.

Signal for a stop or sudden decrease in speed: Hand and arm extended downward beyond the side of the vehicle.

Legislators apparently realize that stops are sometimes made in response to sudden movements of the vehicle or vehicles ahead and do not require any specified duration for the stopping signal. However, these same lawmakers note that turning movements are usually deliberate actions of a motorist, so they require a specified duration to signals required for turning movements. Any signal of intention to turn right or left shall be given continuously during the last one hundred feet traveled by the vehicle before turning.

Right-of-Way

Despite carefully worded provisions of vehicle codes, the right-of-way is still confusing to most motorists, and there is little understanding of the safeguards established by traffic regulations for the guidance of drivers. It is probably an area of traffic control that requires greater education of motorists to secure voluntary compliance. Many road users either do not read or fail to comprehend the vehicle code sections on right-of-way, or they knowingly disregard right-of-way rules.

Right-of-way: Left Turns. Head-on, left-turn collisions involving vehicles approaching each other from opposing directions constitute a major segment of right-of-way accidents. Left-turn directional arrows on traffic signals and modern left-turn storage lanes have reduced this type of accident at signalized intersections. On the other hand, vehicles turning left between intersections (into an alley or public or private property) or at intersections lacking specific control of left-turning and approaching vehicles are frequently involved in left-turn, head-on collisions.

The California Vehicle Code attempts to legislate this right-of-way under the doctrine of *immediate hazard:*

1. The driver of a vehicle intending to turn to the left at an intersection or into public or private property or an alley shall yield the right-of-way to all vehicles which have approached or are approaching from the opposite direction and which are so close as to constitute a hazard at any time during the turning movement and shall continue to yield the right-of-way to such vehicles until such time as the left turn can be made with reasonable safety.
2. A driver having so yielded and giving the required signal may

turn left, and the drivers of all other vehicles approaching from the opposite direction shall yield the right-of-way.

Multilane highways have developed another factor in the right-of-way of vehicles turning left, and this is the fact that approaching vehicles in each lane of a multilane highway must be considered as to their immediacy of hazard before the turning driver crosses each lane and challenges the right-of-way of the approaching vehicle.

Right-of-Way: Signalized Intersections. A signalized intersection is an intersection at which the conflict between vehicles moving at right angles to each other, or any other angle, is controlled by an official traffic control signal: any device, whether manually, electrically, or mechanically operated, by which traffic is alternately directed to stop and proceed. The vehicle facing the green signal, light, or arrow, has the right-of-way in the direction indicated; vehicles in opposing traffic must wait for a signal indicating it is safe for them to proceed.

As a general rule, a driver who enters the intersection lawfully (during a green or "go" signal, or an amber or "caution" signal) may assume that cross traffic will not endanger him by violating a red or "stop" signal, but when danger is apparent to a person of ordinary prudence in the same situation, he is not excused from exercising ordinary care to avoid a collision, even though the danger is created by one who enters or appears about to enter the intersection against a red or "stop" signal.

Right-of-Way: Controlled Intersections. An intersection with some form of regulatory control differs from an uncontrolled intersection in that the right-of-way is subject to the controlling device, usually stop or yield signs, or both. Insofar as right-of-way hazards are concerned, it is not in the class of a signalized intersection in which the signal grants the right-of-way to opposing traffic.

Accidents occur at these locations because of impatience or misunderstanding. The driver about to enter or cross the intersecting roadway underestimates the speed or apparent distance of the approaching vehicle and shortcuts his judgment as to such vehicle's constituting an immediate hazard, or the approaching driver fails to understand that the driver of the vehicle about to enter or cross the roadway has "earned" his right-of-way by stopping and allowing other vehicles constituting an immediate hazard to pass by. The doctrine that drivers of vehicles approaching a controlled intersection should not enter or cross until they can proceed with *reasonable safety* appears to be subordinated to the more nebulous *immediate hazard* concept.

Police action against any driver for failing to yield the right-of-way at a controlled intersection should be based upon three major factors: (1) the driver's obedience to control signs ("Stop" or "Yield"), (2) the driver's perception and judgment as to *immediate hazard,* and (3) the driver's conclusion that he/she could proceed under the circumstances with *reasonable safety.* Action for violating the right-of-way of another vehicle would be appropriate if the offending driver did not obey a "Stop" or "Yield" sign or, after doing so, failed to judge the circumstances of *immediate hazard* and *reasonable safety* as would a reasonable and prudent man under similar circumstances.

The provisions of any Vehicle Code assign the right-of-way at controlled intersections as follows:

Stop Signs: When an intersection is controlled by a stop sign (or a flashing red signal), the driver of any vehicle approaching such stop sign shall stop at the limit line (if marked) before entering the cross-walk on the near side of the intersection or at the "entrance" to the intersecting highway; and shall then yield the right-of-way to other vehicles which have approached or are approaching so closely from another roadway as to constitute an immediate hazard and shall continue to yield the right-of-way to such approaching vehicles until such time as he can proceed with reasonable safety. A driver having so yielded may proceed and the drivers of all other approaching vehicles shall yield the right-of-way to the vehicle entering or crossing the intersection.

Yield Signs: When an intersection is controlled by a yield sign (or a flashing amber signal), the driver of any vehicle approaching such yield sign shall yield the right-of-way to other vehicles which have entered the intersection from an intersecting street or which are approaching so closely on the intersecting street as to constitute an immediate hazard and shall continue to yield the right-of-way to such approaching vehicles until such time as he can proceed with reasonable safety. A driver having so yielded may then proceed, and the drivers of all other vehicles approaching the intersection on the intersecting roadway shall yield the right-of-way to him.

Right-of-Way: Uncontrolled Intersection. A large segment of right-of-way accidents are right-angle collisions at uncontrolled intersections:

roadway intersections which are not signalized or controlled by stop or yield signs.

The basic provisions for establishing the right-of-way which will normally prevent such accidents at these intersections, if observed by drivers, are as follows:

1. The driver of a vehicle approaching an intersection shall yield the right-of-way to a vehicle which has entered the intersection from a different highway.
2. When two vehicles enter an intersection from different highways at the same time, the driver of the vehicle on the left shall yield the right-of-way to the driver of the vehicle on his right.

Police action against offending operators requires intelligent observation of the vehicles in motion prior to their conflict and an understanding of this violation. Local courts expect the policeman to testify to his observation and to recall the essential elements of this violation.

Right-of-Way: Not at Intersections. The drivers of vehicles proceeding along highways in California between intersections have a substantial right-of-way as opposed to drivers about to enter or cross a highway from an alley, or from public or private property (driveways or entrances or exits from such public or private property): The driver of a vehicle about to enter or cross a highway from any public or private property or from an alley shall yield the right-of-way to all vehicles approaching on the highway.

Right-of-Way: School Crosswalks. When children must cross a roadway on their way to and from school and the crossing is not at a signalized or controlled intersection, local regulations usually provide for erection of signs such as *"School Xing—Stop When Occupied," "Slow—School Zone,"* or *"Slow—School Xing."* The erection of such signs is warranted by the facts and circumstances of the location and its traffic volume, with the overriding consideration being the protection and safety of children attending school.

Right-of-Way: Authorized Emergency Vehicles. A substantial right-of-way is provided in vehicle codes for authorized emergency vehicles. Drivers of other vehicles, upon the immediate approach of an authorized emergency vehicle sounding a siren and having at least one red light (normally visible to the front of the vehicle), must yield the right-of-way and move to positions out of the path of the approaching emergency vehicle and remain there until it has passed.

Speed Restrictions

A vehicle code may limit speed through either an absolute speed restriction or by establishing a *prima facie** speed law. Many states— including California—utilize both restrictions. Regulations that set certain fixed speed limits and state that any speed in excess of these limits is unlawful are termed *absolute speed restrictions;* the *prima facie* restriction is keyed to a provision that speeds in excess of a basic speed law are unlawful. Some vehicle codes contain a "too fast for conditions" speed restriction. This is also termed an *assured clear distance* rule. Its provisions require motorists to maintain control of their vehicles at all times under all conditions, not driving at a greater speed than will permit bringing the vehicle to a stop within the assured clear distance ahead.

California's Vehicle Code has an easily understood statement of speed law violations and utilizes absolute, "too fast for conditions," and *prima facie* restrictions to gain effective speed control on its highways. These laws are worded substantially as follows:

1. **Maximum Speed Law:** No person shall drive a vehicle upon a highway at a speed greater than 65 mph except on specially designated freeways upon which signs have been erected permitting a higher maximum speed limit of 70 mph. The speed of any vehicle upon a highway in excess of the authorized speed limit is unlawful unless the defendant establishes by competent evidence that the speed in excess of said limits did not constitute a violation of the basic speed law at the time, place, and under the conditions then existing.

    A. **Temporary Maximum Speed Limit.** Notwithstanding other provisions of this Code to the contrary, no person shall drive a vehicle upon a highway at a speed greater than 55 mph.

2. **Basic Speed Laws:** No person shall drive a vehicle upon a highway at a speed greater than is reasonable or prudent, having due regard for weather, visibility, the traffic on and the surface and width of the highway, and in no event at a speed which endangers the safety of persons or property.

3. **Prima Facie Speed Limits:** Vehicles shall not be operated in excess of posted speed limits in certain places and circumstances. RR

---

*On the face of: uncontradicted. (See Glossary for "words and phrases".)

Xing, alley, limited-view intersection, highway-work area, and under snow and ice conditions.

4. **Special Speed Limits:** The California Vehicle Code sets a maximum speed for designated trucks and other vehicles, lowers such speed for some of these vehicles when unsafe because of grades, permits variable speed limits for highways and roadways of multi-lane divided highways, allows for different speed limits in adjoining lanes of traffic, and establishes a minimum speed law.

Prosecutions for Speed Violations. Most prosecutions for violations of vehicle code restrictions related to speed are for violations of the maximum or posted speed limits. Prosecutions for violating the basic speed law (too fast for conditions) are generally associated with accidents indicating one or more of the drivers of the vehicles involved violated this law, or gross and flagrant violations of reasonable and prudent speed limits when weather conditions such as rain, snow, ice or fog make driving hazardous. Prosecutions for driving too slow may be related to behavior on the highway indicating the vehicle is almost a roadway obstruction or in areas posted for minimum speeds.

In the prosecution of violators of vehicle code restrictions on speed an officer is required to testify to two major points of evidence, that (1) the defendant was in fact the operator of the car the officer observed and (2) the car the officer observed was violating the speed restriction specified in the local vehicle code.

The identification of the defendant as the operator of the car is generally an uncomplicated procedure for the police witness. Usually the prosecutor will ask a bland question as to whether or not the officer can identify this person; when the officer answers in the affirmative, the prosecutor requests that the witness point out the person in the courtroom. Lengthy continuances in cases involving members of motorcycle police units often complicated this point of evidence. These police officers frequently served from twenty to twenty-five speeding citations in a day, and when trial postponement extended the normal time for trial, it was not unusual to encounter a problem with identification of offenders.

Identification of the defendant as the driver of the vehicle concerned may often be a problem when the speed section of the vehicle code charged is related to "too fast for conditions" and involves an accident. Officers do not usually observe the offender operating the vehicle in such instances. However, many states permit a prosecutor to develop this identification through witnesses other than the police officer.

Testimony regarding the speed of the vehicle is the core area of these cases and therefore is a vital area for cross-examination. A defense attorney can win an acquittal for his client on cross-examination. Officers should never presume that a defendant will not be represented by counsel.

Years ago, a nonspecific method of determining speed such as an "eyeball clock" might withstand cross-examination. An officer was permitted to testify that in his opinion the defendant was speeding. The officer had watched the driver approach his position along the highway, noted his speed was above the maximum limit and flagged him down. Of course, the officer testified that he or she had certain skills in this area due to work experience in traffic, but this was about as specific evidence was required of such testimony in past years.

Today police utilize equipment to "clock" speeders. It may be radar is some states or aircraft in others, but the most common device among available equipment is the speedometer of the police vehicle. It is vital to police action in these speed violation cases that the officer can testify to an official test within a reasonable time by qualified experts as to the accuracy of such equipment in measuring speed. The prosecutor may be required to produce such an expert and the testing equipment; many courts seek a stipulation from a defense counsel to this effect in recognition of the integrity of police supervisors and their selection of such qualified persons and equipment.

Many police units require excessive speed to be clocked over a minimum distance. Some police officials are reluctant to approve touch-and-go procedures because they expose the police action to the defense plea that the excessive speed was only momentary or was only a result of an attempt of the defendant to avoid an accident or to safely complete a passing maneuver. While the downgrade of many access roads will assist the acceleration of the police vehicle, it is often difficult for a police officer to push his vehicle to an equal speed with the violator before the normally distinctive silhouette of the police vehicle is spotted in the rearview mirror of the violator and any opportunity for formal "pacing" is ruined.

Courts will permit an officer to testify to his closing speed with the violator and the difficulty experienced by the police witness in closing the gap between the two cars. This can be given in seconds or highway distance. Most courts insist that during the clock, whatever its nature, that the offending vehicle was not lost to the sight of the pursuing officer. This is necessary to protect the integrity of the speeding observation by the officer.

On cross-examination, the officer may be questioned about sight distances on curves and "dips" in the highway. A momentary loss of line-of-sight between the two cars does not necessarily ruin the credibility of the officer's testimony and thereby create a reasonable doubt of the offender's guilt and a dismissal or acquittal in the case, but it does arm the cross-examiner with an area for further questioning directed toward the opportunity for mistake or accident. The officer might have pulled over a vehicle similar in size and shape to the one he had pursued and clocked instead of the offending car. Almost any amount of traffic on the highway supports this area of questioning, and it is difficult for the officer to prove that the car he stopped was the one he chased if it was out of his view for a short time.

Reckless Driving

The words of vehicle codes from state to state may vary slightly in defining reckless or dangerous driving, but the meaning and legislative intent of such code sections is the same in any state. Each of the statutes forbidding reckless driving has the same basic purpose of stopping dangerous and criminal driving. In some states a citation can be served for reckless driving whenever the driver's conduct results in an accident, after a trained and experienced police officer has reviewed the facts of the accident. In others, it is necessary that such conduct be within the circumstances stipulated in the vehicle code section dealing with reckless driving. Successive offenses or resultant injury usually adds to the sanctions imposed for this violation.

California's reckless driving section is an "open end" section in that it stipulates conduct sufficiently broad to be applied in many accident situations in which such driving is the major cause of the tragedy. It defines the reckless driver as "any person who drives any vehicle upon a highway in willful and wanton disregard for the safety of persons and property." When reckless drivers are cited in connection with an accident and the driving "proximately causes bodily injury to any person," the possible punishment upon conviction is increased to six months from the basic maximum sentence for reckless driving of ninety days; the possible fine is upped from 250 to 500 dollars.

Reckless driving is more than mere negligence; it is a failure to perform because of carelessness, oversight, or failure to act in a manner common to a "reasonable and prudent" operator of a vehicle. Officers must be in a position to testify that the cited or arrested operator's driving had inherent characteristics of a wanton disregard of the consequences which might ensue from the act or the failure to act. Relevant and material testimony would hew to the theme that such driving unreasonably interfered with the free and proper use of a public highway or unreasonably endangered the users of such public highway.

Officers testifying in court in such cases do not have to give evidence showing that the cited or arrested operator charged with reckless driving intentionally caused bodily injury or property damage, or even that the driver recognized the hazardous potentiality of his conduct. It is usually sufficient if the officer brings to court evidence which will prove that the offender's driving was "conscious and intentional driving which the driver knows, or should know, creates an unreasonable risk of harm to others."

Speed contests are considered reckless driving in many states. Unbelievably, the ordinary "dragging" utilizing a traffic signal device to start the race has been extended to semiformal contests in which barricades are unlawfully placed on the highway to facilitate the speed contest. In California, persons engaging in speed contests are liable to punishment equal to that of reckless driving.

"Moving" Violations

"Moving" violations identify sections of a vehicle code in which the vehicle is in motion under the control of a driver, as opposed to code sections concerned with parking and vehicle equipment. It isolates the infractions likely to result in a traffic accident because such "movers" are believed to be the major factor causing past accidents.

The greatest reenforcement for belief in this relationship are the simple dynamics of many accidents as discovered by police servicing accident scenes. Again and again, it is apparent that "speed kills," reckless driving is just that, no one wins when there is a dispute about the right of way, and drivers recklessly overtaking and passing another vehicle or turning suddenly in the path of an oncoming car or truck apparently wish for death.

Chapter 3

DRIVERS UNDER THE INFLUENCE
OF ALCOHOL OR DRUGS

Drunk driver very aptly describes the boy or girl, woman or man, or senior citizen who drinks and drives. He or she does not have to be a slobbering drunk as long as there are signs of excessive intake of an alcoholic beverage and the suspect driver fails a roadside sobriety test and/or a mandatory chemical test to determine blood alcohol concentration (BAC). The sobriety test indicates the observable signs of intoxication; the chemical test detects the suspect's BAC—and intoxication if measured above legal limits (legal limit for intoxication in most states is 0.10 percent; in California it is 0.08).

Alcohol-related traffic accidents are tragedies, with the accident risk beginning with the initial drink of wine, beer, or whiskey and ending only when the drunk driver reaches his or her destination (see Fig. 4).

Driving under the influence of alcohol (DUI) may be discovered

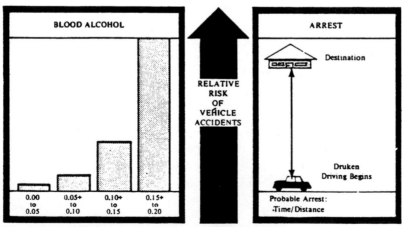

Note: Each bar of blood alcohol graph represents approximately three drinks: 1 oz., 86-proof whiskey; 160-pound person, two hours of eating.

Figure 4. Accident Risk—Drunken Driving: A. Blood-alcohol content: B. Time/Distance.

28

during any traffic accident investigation, or as a result of police observing unsafe driving, making a stop, and encountering a suspected drunken driver.

In recent years, alcohol-related traffic accidents have totaled an unbelievable 1 million a year; the body count each year in fatal accidents of drunk drivers reached 17,000; and total cost of such accidents is figured to be between 25 and 26 billion dollars.

Struggling to gain statistical recognition is the number of drunk drivers saved from impending collisions by the evasive action of other drivers. Police in pursuit of a suspected drunk driver have often watched the suspect car speed through a busy intersection—saved from harm by panic stops of other drivers.

There are too many drunken drivers. Accident data and police reports of DUI arrests only indicates the identified drunks.

There are also too many drivers who mix alcohol and drugs, or men and women who drive under the influence of drugs alone. Chemical tests for blood alcohol concentration are not helpful, nor is sobriety testing. A few drivers admit to drug use, and police officers may assume such use from distinctive scars and marks or the possession of drugs or drug paraphernalia by a driver or found in his or her vehicle. Again, traffic accident records only count arrestees or accident participants identified as driving while under the influence of alcohol and drugs or drugs alone.

DUI Laws

There is a basic uniformity in law making in this area. Intoxicated people operate vehicles unsafely; therefore, anyone who can be classed as a drunk violates specific provisions of law when operating a vehicle. From this base, state laws differ; some vehicle codes provide coverage extending to the possession of or the drinking of intoxicating beverages in a motor vehicle. In recent years, drug use—alone or in conjunction with the intake of alcohol—has been recognized as dangerous and forbidden.

California has an extensive array of laws designed to control the problem of drunken and/or drugged drivers. These laws are: It is unlawful for any person who is under the influence of any alcoholic beverage, or drug, or the combined influence of any alcoholic beverage and drug, to drive a vehicle. It is unlawful for any person who has 0.08 percent or more, by weight, of alcohol in his or her blood to drive a vehicle.*

Drivers under the age of 21, in California and many other states, have more severe restrictions: 0.05 BAC and up is unlawful, and 0.01 BAC and up as measured by a "preliminary screening device" is also unlawful, and the police officer making the stop and giving the test must seize the operator's license of the under-21 driver and serve a suspension order on him or her. After conviction, the youthful driver may have their car (if registered in their name) impounded for up to 30 days—in addition to jail "time," fine, probation, or other penalty.

Most states provide for an escalation of the penalty if the DUI driver injures any other occupant of a vehicle in an accident, is convicted of the same offense a second time, or has repeated offenses within specified time periods.

Causing Injury to Passenger. It is unlawful for any person while under the influence of any alcoholic beverage or drug, or the combined influence of any alcoholic beverage and drug, to drive a vehicle and concurrently do any act forbidden by law, or neglect any duty imposed by law in driving a vehicle which act or neglect proximately causes bodily injury to any person other than the driver. The act or neglect does not need to be any specific section of the vehicle code. Mandatory sentence on first offense requires county jail imprisonment for 96 hours and allows up to six months and a fine from 400 to 1000 dollars (a severe penalty when compared to the open-end first-offender DUI sentence of hours in the county jail, less than 1000 dollar fine, probation, and possible license suspension).

Penalty for DUI Repeat Offenders. If any person is again convicted of a second DUI offense within seven years of his or her original conviction, he or she may expect a severe sentence: 90 days to 1 year in county jail or probation requiring: (1) 10-days to 1 year in county jail, a fine of 400–1000 dollars, and suspension of driver's license; or (2) 48 hours to 1 year in county jail, a fine of 400–1000 dollars, and some form of community service or driver training.

Drivers convicted of their third and subsequent offense in seven years are in deep trouble: longer period in county jail, revocation of driver's license, and identification as a habitual traffic violator. The penalty for

*California Vehicle Code, Article 2, "Offenses Involving Alcohol and Drugs", Section 23152 *et seq.*

fourth offenders suggests state prison terms or probation with concurrent sentence to a county jail.

For too many years, and in too many states, prosecutors have used the "misdemeanor murder" provisions of a vehicle code to charge and try drunks clearly responsible for the death of one or more people in a traffic collision. Uniformly, relatives and friends of the victim(s) have been screaming at the sentencing judge for a sentence of less than ten years—despite the judge's explanation that this term was the maximum for the vehicle manslaughter conviction.

For instance, in New Mexico, on Christmas Eve, a wrong-way DUI driver killed a woman and her three daughters in a head-on collision. The 36-year-old male DUI took the chemical test a half-hour after the accident and tested out at 0.18 BAC. Two years and two mistrials later, the DUI driver was convicted of four counts of vehicle manslaughter. The judge has accepted the jury verdict and all concerned are awaiting the sentencing. The judge, however, is bound by the "max" limits of New Mexico law; the victim's family and friends want nothing less than a life or death sentence.

Detection and Apprehension of Drunken Drivers

Detection of the driver who is under the influence of alcohol is usually initiated in one of three ways:

1. As a result of a call to the scene of an accident.
2. As the result of stopping the individual for an infraction of a driving rule, or as a result of a check of loads, lights, equipment, operator's license, etc.
3. Personal observation of the individual while he/she is driving a vehicle.

The external evidence of the presence of alcohol in a person suspected of being under the influence of alcohol relies upon visual and other senses to note the behavior and condition of the suspect. When such activity deviates from what would be expected of a sober person under like circumstances, it is significant.

When called to the scene of an accident and discovering a suspect drunken driver, or finding a suspect drunken driver when the officer stops a motorist for another reason, the officer begins his observation from the first indication of drunkenness.

The first observation of the suspect driver that has alerted the officer to the possibility of drunken driving is important. Is it the driving behavior? Is it behavior at an accident scene? What was first noticed as unusual or deviant behavior? Where was the observing officer at the time? What was the officer doing? What time of day was it? What were the light and weather conditions?

Drivers operating their vehicles in any manner which would raise a doubt as to their sobriety or other abnormal condition should be stopped and the cause for the erratic driving ascertained. A few examples of deviations from normal driving, for which the officer must be alert, are:

1. Speed where geographical characteristics or other circumstances would ordinarily compel a slower speed.
2. Excessive speed, with frequent lane changing.
3. Driving in spurts, first slow and then fast, or vice versa.
4. Driving unreasonably slow.
5. Weaving from road edge to lane or center line; sharp, jerky movements in correcting direction of travel; overcontrolling.
6. Driving too close to or striking curbs (touch and go), or appearing to hug the shoulder or center of the roadway, or continually straddling the center line or lane markings.
7. Improper passing without sufficient clearance or sudden cutting in; taking too long or swerving too much in overtaking and passing; overcontrolling.
8. Overshooting or disregarding traffic signs or signals.
9. Approaching signs or signals too fast or slow; stopping or attempting to stop with uneven motions.
10. Unnecessary use of turn indicators.
11. Driving at night without lights or with parking lights only; delay in turning lights on.
12. Failure to dim lights when approaching traffic repeatedly indicates to the suspect that his lights are on bright or "high beam."
13. Jerky starting or stopping.
14. Driving in lower gears without apparent cause; repeatedly meshing or clashing gears.
15. Driving with windows rolled down in cold weather.
16. Driving or riding with head out of window (partly or completely).

Once a driver is observed as a suspected drunken driver, every reasonable effort should be promptly made to stop him/her at a safe place and remove him/her from the highway until the investigation is completed.

The second period of police observation extends from the time the suspect driver was first alerted to the presence of police, usually by siren and red light, and the time the suspect driver stopped his or her car. All behavior during this period of time is important. This is a follow-up to "first notice" behavior.

Some of the reactions observed during this stage of apprehension are:

1. An unusually fast compliance to the red light and siren; a so-called "screeching halt" or "throwing out the anchor," either on or off the roadway.
2. A slowness or hesitancy to comply to red light and siren.
3. An attempt to ignore or outrun the patrol vehicle.
4. Overuse of arm or directional signals as the vehicle is being stopped.
5. Unusual moving about of the occupant within the vehicle. (There may be an attempted change of drivers while the vehicle is still in motion.)

The third observation period is from the time the officer exited the police car and approached the suspect driver's stopped car, through any sobriety testing, to and including the release of the driver, or his/her arrest and "booking" at the local jail. In many jurisdictions police officers may testify to the refusal of the suspect driver to participate in chemical tests to determine blood alcohol concentration.

During the third period of observation, the officer must search for, and be alert to, any signs indicating the defendant is ill rather than under the influence of alcohol. Appropriate action in the event of illness ranges from first aid to prompt medical attention.

In this external examination of a suspect driver, the officer should determine the suspect's ability to coordinate his or her faculties (at the location where he is apprehended). The officer should supplement general observations by noting specific actions, such as ability to walk, ability to stand, as well as speech, odor of breath, tremor of hands, condition of hair, condition of eyes, color of face, marks or injuries, general appearance, and unusual acts (throwing up, going to sleep, falling down, etc.).

It is during this third observation period that sobriety tests are usually administered, unless the suspect driver is obviously drunk and cannot perform coordination tests. The key facts to be noted, basically, are the tests the suspect driver was asked to perform, and how he or she performed, or if he or she refused to cooperate in these tests.

Sobriety Tests

Sobriety tests measure general coordination. The tests should not be so complicated or difficult that the average person could not perform them when *not* drinking. Simple sobriety tests are:

1. *Finger to Nose:*
    a. Subject stands erect with feet together, eyes closed, and arms outstretched. Alternating left hand and right hand, under the direction of the officer, the subject swings forearm in from the elbow, attempting to touch the tip of the nose with the tip of the extended index finger.
    b. Test is to determine the ability to coordinate movements (touching tip of nose with fingertips), retain balance, and follow simple directions.
2. *Modified Position of Attention:*
    a. Subject stands at "attention," heels and toes together, eyes closed, and head tilted back slightly.
    b. Test is to determine the ability to retain balance.
3. *Heel to Toe:*
    a. Subject is directed to walk in a straight line, placing one foot before the other in a heel-against-toe position.
    b. Test is to determine the ability to place heel against toe, maintain a straight course, and retain balance.
4. *Walking a Straight Line:*
    a. Subject is directed to walk to a specified object, turn and return, or walk along a straight line.
    b. Test is to determine the ability to maintain a straight course, turn smoothly, and retain balance.
5. *Standing on Line:*
    a. Subject is directed to stand in a heel-to-toe position.
    b. Test is to determine the ability to retain balance.
6. *Dexterity—Finger Count:*
    a. Subject is directed to count on his fingers: touch his first finger to his thumb, and count "one," then touch his middle

finger to his thumb and count "two," then the third finger to the thumb and count "three," and—lastly—the little finger to the thumb and count "four." The order may then be reversed: 4, 3, 2, and 1.

b. Test is to determine the ability to coordinate finger movements and speech.

7. *Dexterity—Picking Up Coins:*

a. Place coins (or similar object) on hood of car in front of subject within reaching distance; have subject reach out, pick object up, and place in officer's hand.

b. Test is to determine degree of deviation from the ability of sober person to accomplish the same act.

Each coordination test should be fully explained and demonstrated to the suspect driver in such a manner that he or she understands just what is expected prior to asking the suspect to perform the test.

Many jurisdictions have space on their "Intoxication Report," the form used in drunken driving arrests, to indicate graphically the walking-line test, and the finger-to-nose test. Two straight lines and the outline of a face are provided along with standard symbols for right foot, left foot, and both the right and left index fingers.

The reaction of a suspect driver's eye to light has often been included among sobriety tests. The officer flashing a flashlight in the suspect's eye and either testifying to his own knowledge of a sober person's eye reaction as compared to an intoxicated person's reaction, or putting another officer known to be sober to the test at the scene and reporting the difference in eye reactions to light. However, skilled cross-examination by defense counsels as to the officer's qualifications as an expert on the human eye has revealed police as nonexperts, and this practice is no longer effective or popular.

Arrests—DUI

The officer stopping the suspect driver should not allow the suspect to drive any vehicle until exonerated of any suspicion that driving ability has been impaired by alcohol or illness, nor expose the suspect driver to any roadway hazard during this period of observation. If exonerated, the suspect should be so advised and aided in getting his or her vehicle back into the traffic stream.

After the sobriety test, if the officer's decision is to make a DUI arrest, he or she shall so inform the subject, search for weapons or harmful objects, handcuff him or her, and transport the arrestee as quickly as possible to the police premises wherein the chemical testing may be conducted.

An arrest can be made after an accident by a peace officer, without a warrant, when the suspect is involved in the traffic accident or is observed by the officer in or about a vehicle obstructing the roadway, when the officer has reasonable cause to believe such person has been driving under the influence of intoxicating liquor and any drug. When a DUI arrest is made at the scene of an accident, normal procedures may have to be subordinated to medical care for the arrestee.

Local rules will indicate the forms necessary to the arrest and booking of any arrestee and the "Officer's Statement" required in DUI cases (see Fig. 5).

Of particular importance in the officer's statement are the segments titled: "Probable Cause" and "Objective Symptoms." Together they should contain a summing up of all justification for the arrest.

The "Implied Consent" Law and Chemical Testing

The intent of the implied consent law now in effect in most jurisdictions is to aid in the determination of guilt or innocence in criminal prosecutions in which the defendant is accused of driving a motor vehicle when under the influence of alcohol. This law aids police in securing an offender's permission to participate in a chemical test to determine his or her blood alcohol concentration. For this reason, chemical tests for blood alcohol concentration are incidental to a lawful arrest developed by the arresting officer from personal observation, sobriety tests, interviews with witnesses, and other available evidence.

In California the "implied consent law" reads:

(a) Any person who drives a motor vehicle upon a highway shall be deemed to have given consent to a chemical test of his or her blood, breath, or urine for the purpose of determining the alcoholic content of his or her blood if lawfully arrested for any offense allegedly committed while the person was driving a motor vehicle under the influence of intoxicating liquor. The test shall be incidental to a lawful arrest and administered at the direction of a peace officer having reasonable cause to believe such person was driving a motor vehicle upon a highway while under the influence of intoxicating liquor. Such person shall be told that failure to submit to or complete such a chemical test will result in suspension of his or her privilege to operate a motor vehicle for a period of six months.

OFFICER'S STATEMENT

SECTIONS 13353.1, 13353.2 AND 13353 VEHICLE CODE

DMV
A Public Service Agency

☐ **BAC 0.01** (Under Age 21) ☐ **BAC 0.05** (Under Age 21) ☐ **BAC 0.08** (Any Age) ☐ **REFUSAL** (Complete reverse side)

LAW ENFORCEMENT AGENCY CASE NUMBER

FORWARD THIS FORM TO YOUR LOCAL DRIVER SAFETY OFFICE WITHIN 5 BUSINESS DAYS. (Complete in black ink.) Telephone No. (916) 657-7730

DRIVER LICENSE NUMBER STATE

NAME (LAST, FIRST, M.I.) DOB **RIGHT THUMB PRINT**

MAILING ADDRESS STATE ZIP CODE

NOTE: PLEASE COMPLETE PHYSICAL DESCRIPTION OF DRIVER:

Sex: Age: Hair: Eyes: Ht.: Wt.:

Vehicle License No. _____ ☐ Violation occurred in a vehicle requiring a commercial driver license (Section 15210 VC).

On _____ at _____ AM/PM in _____ CA, the above named driver was

☐ **observed driving by** ☐ this officer ☐ the observer shown below ☐ **in or about a vehicle blocking a roadway** under Section 40300.5 VC

☐ **involved in a collision** (state how time of collision was established or attach collision report.)

I had reasonable cause to believe the driver was driving a motor vehicle while under the influence, or while under age 21 with alcohol present in the blood. The **driver was detained/arrested on** _____ at _____ AM/PM for violation of Vehicle Code Section 23136, 23140, 23152 or **23153 (including Section 191.5[a] and 192[c] of the Penal Code).**

PROBABLE CAUSE for stop or contact. Please **describe in detail** the facts and circumstances that led to the stop or contact: _____

Objective symptoms of intoxication ☐ Bloodshot/watery eyes ☐ Odor of alcoholic beverage ☐ Unsteady gait ☐ Slurred speech
☐ Other _____

☐ Driving observed ☐ Arrested ☐ Citizen's arrest ☐ Collision wit. by | ☐ Driving observed ☐ Arrested ☐ Citizen's arrest ☐ Collision wit. by

CITIZEN'S/OFFICER'S NAME/ID NUMBER | CITIZEN'S/OFFICER'S NAME/ID NUMBER

ADDRESS/AGENCY | ADDRESS/AGENCY

TELEPHONE NUMBER ( ) | TELEPHONE NUMBER ( )

PRELIMINARY ALCOHOL SCREENING TEST 0.01 BAC SUSPENSION Under Age 21 (23137/13353.2 VC)

Driver submitted to and completed a preliminary alcohol screening test with results of: Test 1 ____ BAC Test 2 ____ BAC *(optional)*

TEST 1 _____ at _____ AM/PM TEST 2 _____ at _____ AM/PM

I certify under penalty of perjury under the laws of the State of California, that the PAS test device was in proper working condition and the results were obtained in the regular course of my duties.

Date _____ Signature **X** _____ ID _____ Agency/Div. _____

0.05 BAC UNDER AGE 21 or 0.08 BAC SUSPENSION (13353.2 VC) Submit blood/urine test results within 15 days.

☐ Blood Date _____ Time _____ AM/PM
☐ Urine Date _____ Time of First Void _____ AM/PM Time of Test _____ Results _____

BREATH TEST RESULTS *(Attach a copy of the results.)*

TEST 1 _____ at _____ AM/PM Results _____ TEST 2 _____ at _____ AM/PM Results _____
TEST 3 _____ at _____ AM/PM Results _____

BREATH TEST MACHINE OPERATOR'S CERTIFICATION

I certify under penalty of perjury under the laws of the State of California, that the above breath test sample results were obtained in the regular course of my duties. I further certify that I am qualified to operate this equipment and that the test was administered pursuant to the requirements of Title 17 of the California Code of Regulations.

Date _____ Signature **X** _____ ID _____ Agency/Div. _____

☐ DS 360 Suspension/Revocation Order was issued (Please Attach) | ☐ Suspension/Revocation Order was *not* issued
☐ DS 360A Suspension/Revocation Order was issued (Please Attach) | ☐ Driver license was confiscated (Please Attach)

NAME OF OFFICER (PLEASE PRINT) BADGE/ID NO.

AGENCY AREA PHONE NO. ( )

Executed at _____ CITY _____ COUNTY _____ STATE on _____ DATE

I certify under penalty of perjury, under the laws of the State of California, that the information on both sides of this form is true and correct.

Signature of Officer **X** _____

DS 367 (REV. 4/95)

Figure 5. California's Department of Motor Vehicles (DMV) "Officer's Statement" form prepared in all DUI cases by the arresting officer. The "Probable Cause" and "Objective Symptoms" segments, when filled in by the officer, should justify the DUI arrest. The reverse side of this form focuses on the chemical test for DUI.

The person arrested shall have the choice of whether the test shall be of his blood, breath, or urine, and he or she shall be advised by the officer that he or she has such choice. If the person arrested either is incapable, or states that he or she is incapable, of completing any chosen test, he or she shall then have the choice of submitting to and completing any of the remaining tests, and shall be advised by the officer that he or she has such choice.

Such person shall also be advised by the officer that he or she does not have the right to have an attorney present before stating whether he will submit to a test, before deciding which test to take, or during administration of the test chosen.

Any person who is dead, unconscious, or otherwise in a condition rendering him incapable of refusal shall be deemed not to have withdrawn his consent and such tests may be administered whether or not such person is told that failure to submit to the test will result in the suspension of his privilege to operate a motor vehicle.

(b) If any such person refuses the officer's request to submit to or fails to complete, a chemical test, the department (DMV), upon receipt of the officer's sworn statement that he had reasonable cause to believe such person had been driving a motor vehicle upon a highway while under the influence of intoxicating liquor and that the person had refused to submit to, or failed to complete, the test after being requested by the officer, shall suspend his privilege to operate a motor vehicle for a period of six months.

No such suspension shall become effective until ten days after the giving of written notice thereof, as provided for in subdivision (c).

(c) The department (DMV) shall immediately notify such person in writing of the action taken and upon his request in writing and within fifteen days from the date of receipt of such request shall afford him an opportunity for a hearing.

Police officers do not give the *Miranda* warning in DUI cases until the chemical test admonishment is given, and the suspect understands this admonishment and makes his or her decision about taking the chemical test. Roadside questioning of a motorist detained in a routine traffic stop does not constitute "custodial interrogation."[*]

In addition, the presumption that a dead-unconscious-whatever person can be given the chemical test has been criticized—whenever evidence is taken from a person without their consent it is a violation of their V–Amendment protection against self-incrimination and IV–Amendment safeguard against illegal searches. Leading court decisions, however, support an opposing viewpoint. The United States Supreme

---

[*]Daniel T. Gilbert, "What Powers Do Police Have at Traffic Stops?" *Traffic Safety*, Vol. 95, No. 1 (January/February 1995), 26–27.

Court in *Breithaupt v. Abram,* 352 U.S. 432 (1957), said human blood was a nontestimonial body substance and not within the Fifth Amendment's protection against self-incrimination. In *Schmerber v. California,* 384 U.S. 757 (1966), the United States Supreme Court held that the extraction of a body fluid for chemical analysis or the body fluid itself was neither an unreasonable search or compelled testimony.

Chemical Test Procedures

The arresting officer, in cases of driving a motor vehicle while under the influence of alcohol, will be expected to testify in court at the trial of the offender as to his or her role in administering the chemical test and the chain of possession of the evidence sample. The officer is not expected to testify as an expert as to any interpretation of the results of this testing.

In some jurisdictions, as an economy measure, the blood, urine, and breath samples are submitted for analysis only when the defendant enters a plea of not guilty. These jurisdictions, however, direct the agency in which the evidence samples are placed for safekeeping not to discard them upon a guilty plea by a defendant. There are many cases in which the defendant has entered a plea of guilty, then at a later date applied to court for permission to vacate this plea and enter a new plea of not guilty. Retention of these samples should be for a reasonable time after the case has been concluded with judgment and sentence.

In California, the Vehicle Code establishes the following procedures for chemical tests to determine blood-alcohol concentration:

(a) Only a physician, registered nurse, licensed vocational nurse, or duly licensed clinical laboratory technologist or clinical laboratory bioanalyst acting at the request of a peace officer may withdraw blood for the purpose of determining the alcoholic content therein. This limitation shall not apply to the taking of breath specimens.

(b) The person tested may, at his own expense, have a physician, registered nurse, licensed vocational nurse, duly licensed clinical laboratory technologist or clinical laboratory bioanalyst, or any other person of their own choosing administer a test, in addition to any administered at the direction of a peace officer, for the purpose of determining the amount of alcohol in their blood at the time alleged as shown by chemical analysis of their blood, breath, or urine. The failure or inability to obtain an additional test by a person shall not preclude the admissibility in evidence of the test taken at the direction of a peace officer.

(c) Upon the request of the person tested, full information concerning the test taken at the direction of the peace officer shall be made available to defendant and his or her attorney.

Procedural regulations in California administrative law has established the following regulations for chemical testing for alcohol in breath, urine, and blood:

Breath: Breath-alcohol test instruments may be operated by peace officers, providing the instrument is under the direct jurisdiction of a governmental agency or a licensed forensic alcohol laboratory. A breath-alcohol instrument is a device that actually analyzes a sample of breath for its alcohol content. All breath-alcohol instruments used shall be of a type approved by the Department of Public Health.

A breath sample shall be essentially alveolar in composition (deep lung breath). The sample shall be collected only after the subject has been under continuous observation for at least fifteen minutes. During the fifteen-minute observation period the subject shall not be permitted to ingest alcoholic beverages or other fluids, eat, or smoke. If he or she should regurgitate during this time, administering the test shall be delayed for another fifteen-minute observation period.

Officers who operate breath-alcohol instruments must have been trained in the operation of such instruments. Such training must be under the supervision of persons who qualify as forensic alcohol analysts in a licensed forensic alcohol laboratory. Minimum training shall include the theory of operation, detailed procedure of operation, practical experience, precautionary checklist, and a written or practical examination, or both.

Urine: The only approved urine sample shall be a sample collected no sooner than twenty minutes after having the suspect driver void his bladder. A clean, dry container, containing a preservative, shall be used for this sample. A portion of the urine sample is required to be retained to satisfy the discovery rights of the defendant (access to evidence against him). In some jurisdictions a sample of the first bladder voiding is collected for tests related to drugs. The suspect driver electing to have a urine test should be informed prior to testing that the test consists of (1) voiding his bladder and, (2) twenty to thirty minutes later, delivering a test sample of adequate quantity.

Blood: Blood samples are to be obtained only by authorized persons (physician, registered nurse, licensed vocational nurse, duly licensed clinical laboratory technologist, or clinical laboratory bioanalyst) and in a prescribed manner. A portion of the blood sample is required to be retained to satisfy a possible request by the defense for such sample.

The elaborate procedures of lawmakers, as illustrated by California's example, reveals these chemical tests procedures as safeguarding the intrinsic value of the analysis of the breath, urine, or blood samples as evidence, as well as preserving the integrity and validity of the test for the protection of the accused person.

Presumptive Limits—Blood Alcohol Concentration (BAC)

Where an essential element of the crime charged in drunken driving cases is being "under the influence," there must be proof that the defendant's ability to drive was impaired by the presence of alcohol in his or her blood.

It is not necessary that the driver be "drunk" or "intoxicated," as the law merely provides that such driver shall be "under the influence of intoxicating liquor." If intoxicating liquor has so far affected his nervous system, brain, or muscles as to impair to an appreciable degree his ability to operate the vehicle in a manner like that of an ordinary prudent and cautious man in the full possession of his faculties, using reasonable care and under like conditions, then such driver is under the influence of intoxicating liquor.

A specific statement of proof in drunken driving cases relies upon blood-alcohol concentration (BAC). A basic relationship exists between any alcohol concentration in the blood, urine, saliva, breath, or spinal fluid, and the amount in the brain. The degree of alcoholic effect (driver impairment) is proportionate to the percentage of alcohol in the brain. The amount of alcohol in the brain, as determined by chemical tests, is expressed in terms of the alcohol concentration in blood and is the percent by weight of alcohol in the blood based upon the grams of alcohol per one hundred cubic centimeters of blood.

In New York, a BAC of 0.05 percent, or less, is *prima facie* evidence that driving was not impaired or that the person tested was *not* intoxicated. A BAC of over 0.05 percent and under 0.08 percent, is *prima facie* evidence of impaired ability to drive and relevant evidence of being intoxicated. A BAC level of 0.12 percent, or higher, is illegal *per se*.

The California Vehicle Code contains a provision establishing an evidentiary presumption in cases of driving while under the influence of intoxicating liquor by citing various BAC levels:

(a) Upon the trial of any criminal action, or preliminary proceeding in a criminal action, arising out of acts alleged to have been committed by any person while driving a vehicle while under the influence of intoxicating liquor, the amount of alcohol in the person's blood at the time of the test as shown by chemical analysis of his blood, breath, or urine shall give rise to the following presumptions affecting the burden of proof:

   (1) If there was at that time less than 0.05 percent by weight of alcohol in the person's blood, it shall be presumed that the person was not under the influence of intoxicating liquor at the time of the alleged offense.

(2) If there was at that time 0.5 percent or more but less than 0.08 percent by weight of alcohol in the person's blood, such fact shall not give rise to any presumption that the person was or was not under the influence of intoxicating liquor, but such fact may be considered with other competent evidence in determining whether the person was under the influence of intoxicating liquor at the time of the alleged offense.

(3) If there was at that time 0.08 percent or more by weight of alcohol in the person's blood, it shall be presumed that the person was under the influence of intoxicating liquor at the time of the alleged offense.

(b) Percent by weight of alcohol in the blood shall be based upon grams of alcohol per 100 milliliters of blood.

(c) The foregoing provisions shall not be construed as limiting the introduction of any other competent evidence bearing upon the question whether the person was under the influence of intoxicating liquor at the time of the alleged offense.

There is a strong suspicion among police in California that a BAC of 0.08 percent as a presumptive standard is a liberal interpretation of the condition of the suspect. No injustice to any suspect is involved when the arrested person has a BAC of 0.08 percent or greater, and is presumed to be "under the influence of intoxicating liquor."

The amount of alcohol in the blood depends not only on the amount drunk but also on the weight of the drinker, the kind of alcohol, the time interval since the alcohol was drunk, and whether it was taken with or without food. Age, sex, or previous driving experience is not a factor in an individual's response to alcohol. On the average, researchers agree that alcohol—even in small amounts—affects driving skills, and that driver performance deteriorates as more alcohol is consumed. Deterioration is progressive and linearly related to the BAC.

Drivers Under the Influence of Drugs

Detection and apprehension of persons under the influence of narcotics or dangerous drugs to a degree impairing their ability to drive a vehicle safely is usually associated with the detection and apprehension of drivers under the influence of alcohol. The unusual or deviant driving behavior is the same, as is the external evidence of some form of intoxication. Only the discovery of drugs in the vehicle or exposed by the suspect driver, the needle marks of "hard" drug addition, or the suspect's admission as to drug intake indicate that the case may involve drugs alone or in combination with alcohol.

When evidence in the case warrants an arrest and a chemical test is given the suspect, one or more body fluids will be available for examination. Local procedures vary because chemical testing for drugs has not become as standardized as chemical testing for blood-alcohol levels.

External evidence, observation, and sobriety tests are not specific as to any combining of drugs and alcohol or being under the influence of drugs rather than alcohol.

In general, a broad approach to this problem of drugs and traffic safety may be summed up as follows: If a narcotic or dangerous drug has so far affected the nervous system, brain, or muscles of the driver of a vehicle as to impair to an appreciable degree his or her ability to operate the vehicle in a manner like that of an ordinary prudent man in full possession of his faculties, using reasonable care, and operating a similar vehicle under like conditions, then such driver is under the influence of a narcotic or dangerous drug.

In most jurisdictions, the narcotics or dangerous drug means and includes the following:

1. *Narcotic Drug.* Any drug which contains any quantity of opium, coca leaves, marijuana pethidine (isonipecaine, meperidine), and opiates or their compound manufacture, salt, alkaloid, or derivative, and every substance neither chemically nor physically distinguishable from them and exempted and excepted preparations containing such drugs or their derivatives, by whatever trade name identified and whether produced directly or indirectly by extraction from substances of vegetable origin or independently by means of chemical synthesis or by a combination of extraction and chemical analysis, as the same are designated in the federal narcotic laws and as specified in the administrative rules and regulations on narcotic control as promulgated by the commissioner of health.

2. *Depressant Drug.* Any drug which contains any quantity of barbituric acid or any of the salts of barbituric acid, or any derivative of barbituric acid which had been designated by the commission of health as habit-forming, or any other drug which contains any quantity of a substance which the commissioner of health, after investigation, has found to have, and by regulation designates as having, a potential for abuse because of its depressant effect on the central nervous system.

3. *Stimulant Drug.* Any drug which contains any quantity of amphetamine or any of its optical isomers; any salt of amphetamine or any salt of an optical isomer of amphetamine; or any substance which the commis-

sioner of health, after investigation, has found to be, and by regulation designated as, habit forming because of its stimulant effect of the central nervous system.

4. *Hallucinogenic Drug.* Any drug which contains any quantity of stramonium, mescaline or peyote, lysergic acid, dielhylomide and psilocybin, or any salts or derivative or compounds of any preparations or mixtures thereof.

Law enforcement agencies fielding traffic units will soon have testing devices capable of detecting drivers who are driving under the influence of drugs. Hopefully, these new machines will offer accurate, valid, and reliable detection and measurement of drugs "In Use."

Prosecution—DUI

In court, during the prosecution of cases related to drunk driving or the possession of alcoholic beverages, an officer will be first subjected to direct examination by the prosecutor calling him to the witness stand. The officer will be asked his or her name and occupation, place of employment, and if employed on a certain date and the hours of duty on that day (the day upon which the defendant was arrested).

This is usually followed by a question about whether the officer observed the defendant on that day and at what time and place, and if the observation was related to a vehicle. Once a prosecutor establishes these facts, he has laid the groundwork for the classic question which will bring out the circumstances of the police action: "What did you do then, officer?" The officer's response is an open-ended answer; he will not usually be interrupted unless the prosecutor wishes to include a certain fact or facts in the officer's testimony. Most prosecutors will wait until the officer has told his story and then present a series of questions that will develop the necessary information to support all the essential elements of the charge and establish a *prima facie* case.

Since the officer has arrested the defendant for a charge related to drunk driving or the possession of alcoholic beverages, the court expects testimony to the major point: Was the defendant drunk, or did he possess an alcoholic beverage? No one asks that the officer contribute any more to this court action than what he observed, heard, smelled, or tasted. It is naturally expected by judges and juries that officers in drunk-driving cases will testify as to the defendant's actions that contributed to establishing the reasonable cause upon which the officer based the arrest.

The officer is then subject to cross-examination by the attorney for the defense. Defense counsel, in these cases, attempts to win a favorable verdict for his client by destroying the credibility of the police witness, or the meaningfulness of his or her testimony, or both. The defense counsel may ruin evidence that has appeared most meaningful to the arresting officer: the erratic driving, the failure to "pass" a locality's standard sobriety test (walking a line, finger to nose, etc.), the fumbling through a billfold for a driver's license, the odor of alcohol, and the bloodshot eyes and slurred speech of the suspect.

Cross-examination is an art. Many attorneys are excellent cross-examiners. The destruction of a police witness and his or her testimony may be very meaningful to the outcome of a case, but this is usually avoided by reliance upon two major factors: (1) the officer must continue to testify truthfully and not allow misrecollection, bias, interest, or possibly deceit to contaminate his testimony, and (2) the prosecutor must move in promptly on redirect examination and repair the damage wrought by the defense counsel on cross-examination.

Officers will remain credible witnesses in drunk-driving cases despite a negative answer on cross-examination to a query about whether blood-shot eyes indicate intoxication; others will also remain credible despite a dogged refusal to concede that a person with bloodshot eyes might not be intoxicated. It is not the response to an individual question that tears down a witness in these cases, it is the gradual destruction of the effect of the testimony of the witness toward proving intoxication of the defendant. Despite the form of responses of a witness, the important fact is that the impact of his or her testimony on a judge or jury indicates that the witness acted as a reasonable and prudent trained police officer in making the arrest, and that he has established reasonable cause for his or her action.

In many cross-examinations, the counsel for the defense will attempt to confuse an officer on the witness stand by the difference between a person being *under the influence* and being *intoxicated.* This line of questioning often is intended to commit the police witness to profiling the defendant as being "obviously intoxicated," and then—point by point— showing that the defendant's impairment of manual dexterity, lowered reaction time, poor balance, defective walking ability, slurred speech, bloodshot eyes, and the odor of alcohol on his breath do not total obvious intoxication. Arresting officers may circumscribe their own testimony in this matter of the degree of intoxication because of their selection of superlatives from among the choices offered on most DUI report forms. Officers must keep in mind the relationship between these forms and their testimony (see Fig. 5).

The provisions of the vehicle code do not require an arresting officer to prove obvious intoxication. Driving skill can be seriously impaired without open and notorious drunkenness. Lawmakers recognized this fact when enacting the sections of the vehicle code making it unlawful for any person to operate a vehicle while under the influence of alcohol.

Chemical tests for intoxication support the officer's testimony as to the defendant being under the influence of alcohol, but make no attempt to indicate outward signs of obvious intoxication. Proof that a strong odor of alcohol or like testimony is unnecessary is now available from statistical analysis of blood tests in these cases.

Possession of alcoholic beverages does not involve an officer in an extensive conflict upon cross-examination, because the essential elements do not require an opinion of the officer. The officer can easily answer any questions about what he or she observed.

Drugged drivers, or drivers intoxicated as a result of the intake of a combination of alcohol and narcotics or dangerous drugs, are an emerging problem for prosecutors and police. Direct examination will be concerned primarily with the arresting officer's testimony as to his or her personal observation of the defendant. Cross-examination will probably attempt to place any bizarre behavior in a favorable frame of reference and avoid any grounds for belief the defendant was "stoned" or on a "bad trip."

Sentencing—DUI

Public opinion has encouraged legislators to be tough and they, in response, have enacted new limits on judicial discretion in DUI cases. It is not a menu but rather a schedule of the amount of a fine and the terms of probation, local jail time, and/or incarceration in state prison. Repeat offenders can now expect an escalating severity in their sentences.

Corruption or fraternal feelings for an offender have hardly ever surfaced, but real concern with rehabilitation has been apparent in most sentences. One judge described his frustration: "The defendant has just been convicted of driving under the influence for the eighth time. In the past, this 37-year-old-woman was fined, jailed, her license to drive suspended, and sent to alcohol rehabilitation. At the time of her last arrest she was driving on a suspended license and had a .32 BAC."

"Tough" sentences for repeat DUI individuals order the offenders to serve a specific term in state prison or local jail, to serve a set period in a lock-in institution for alcohol rehabilitation, and have their license to drive revoked. Probation is the identifier of a "soft" sentence. It may include treatment at an outpatient alcohol rehab clinic, an ignition interlock device which if the offender's BAC registers beyond or too close to legal limits turns off the car's ignition, community service, driver education class, and/or suspension of a driver's license. Fines are most likely to hurt the family of a drunken driver, and have little impact on the offender.

Chapter 4

ZERO TOLERANCE—DRIVING
UNDER THE INFLUENCE

The total number of drunken and/or drugged drivers using America's streets and highways is unknown, but is a grim *too many!* We do know how many of these drivers are: (1) involved in accidents, and (2) arrested in transit or at a casual traffic stop. Unfortunately, this is a "fat" number as many arrested drivers escape justice during arrest to conviction proceedings.

"The law is not fair," declared the mother of a 15-year-old daughter killed by a drunken driver. Angry at what she believed to be a light sentence (an 11-year term on a guilty plea, with release possible in less than six years, for a defendant with four prior DUI convictions), she summed up her anger at the criminal justice system. "People who are violating the law know how to work around it, and they do it over and over."

Zero tolerance means: no suspect driver will be given a "wave-off" before or after a sobriety test unless circumstances truly indicate an arrest is not justified; guilty pleas in exchange for reducing the DUI charge to reckless driving will be reduced or stopped entirely; police and prosecutor will do no less than their best effort at trial; and sentencing judges will follow legislative guidelines in sentencing convicted persons.

Arrest Situation—DUI

A situation at a traffic stop for erratic or other driving suggesting DUI, or the circumstances at an accident scene, often dictate an arrest be made. Sometimes, the circumstances are not clear and the decision is discretionary. Ideally, the suspect's actions during a roadside sobriety test should indicate whether or not the suspect is DUI. Chemical tests are primarily evidence-gathering after a decision to arrest has been made.

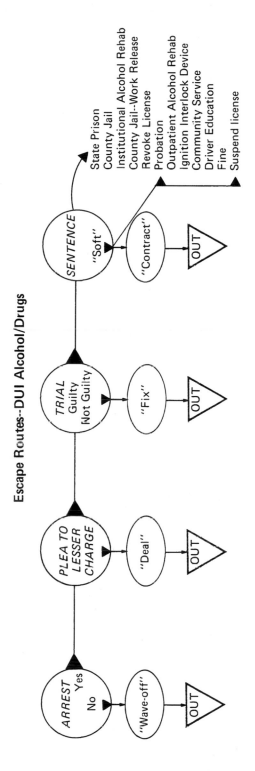

Figure 6. Four major escape routes allow some drivers to escape full responsibility for driving under the influence of alcohol and/or drugs: (1) managing to avoid arrest when an arrest is warranted, (2) negotiating with the prosecution to plead guilty to a lesser charge (reckless driving), (3) by agreeing with prosecutor and/or the arresting officer to give the defendant an "Off" (opportunity for defense to win an aquittal on the issue of guilt or innocence), and (4) persuading the sentencing judge—(when defendant is convicted) to be lenient.

This is truly professional decision making. No colleague or court will be critical, even when the chemical test reports a blood alcohol concentration (BAC) below the legal limit for intoxication. This is the nature of this situation.

Failing to arrest a DUI suspect when an arrest is warranted is disastrously wrong!

Plea Negotiations—DUI

While plea negotiations result in conviction without trial, there is nothing improper in arriving at substantial justice which is agreeable to all parties involved (defendant and counsel, prosecutor, judge) without the time and expense of a trial.*

Traditionally, prosecutors conduct plea negotiations because they are understaffed and courts allow them because of their normal overcrowding. Defense attorneys and their clients seek them to gain a benefit or advantage.

Plea negotiations allowing a guilty plea to a lesser charge in DUI cases are wrong. They are only a means of "beating the rap."

This "out" has been around for years. Most states have revised vehicle codes to prevent misuse of this plea bargaining. California, in 1989, amended Section 2310.6 of its Vehicle Code to place a "tag" on these deals.

1. When the prosecution agrees to a plea of guilty or nolo contendere as a substitute for an original DUI charge, the prosecution must state for the record a factual basis for the substitution and whether or not alcohol and/or drugs were taken by the defendant at the time of the offense.
2. When a court accepts a guilty plea to reckless driving, and the prosecution has filed a statement of alcohol and/or drug use at the time of the original DUI offense, the resulting conviction shall be considered a prior offense for the purposes of the DUI sections of this code—and shall notify the DMV accordingly.

The prior offense citation effectively identifies this reckless driving conviction as being a DUI in legal disguise.

Prosecutors now in a position to make these bargains should curtail or stop them as they are now identifiable as a corrupt procedure illustrative of the misuse of authority.

---

*Paul B. Weston, and Kenneth M. Wells. *Criminal Justice: Introduction and Guidelines* (Pacific Palisades, CA, Goodyear Publishing Company, Inc., 1976), pp. 225–239.

Trial—DUI

The courts trying traffic cases in America are known for fair trials and equal justice, but now and then there are rumors of a "fix" in DUI cases. Facts are hardly ever disclosed, but when the verdict is an acquittal or dismissal, the rumor is reinforced. These suspicions are also encouraged in jurisdictions in which defense attorneys win most of their DUI cases.

No doubt these cases were won because of the skill of legal counsel or the circumstances of the offense, but a nagging suspicion seems to exist as to whether the arresting officer or the prosecutor was "soft" in favor of the defendant. Sometimes, money is mentioned, but most often the motive cited is political favor or fraternal feelings.

Examination of the role of arresting officer and prosecutor in a DUI trial indicates both the possibility and the unlikelihood of a "fix."

Zero tolerance in sentencing is the avoidance of leniency, the use of driver's schools or outpatient alcohol rehabilitation clinics may be a new way of releasing offenders who should be imprisoned (see Figure 6).

Support Program—DUI

Action by police managers likely to support zero-tolerance enforcement of DUI laws is:

1. Short in-service training classes centered on one or more videotapes of a roadside sobriety test in which the decision was to arrest the suspect and a chemical test was taken by the arrestee. In-class discussion should be guided by a class member and aimed at the behavior of the arrestee and his or her BAC level. (This is the "judgment call" training found to be both useful and popular in police firearms training.)

2. In-class discussion sessions led by one of the officers (impromtu selection), and focused on a combination of: (a) reasons given by suspect drunk drivers NOT to make the arrest—and the BAC in the case; and (b) anecdotes of suspect DUI drivers whose conduct dictates an arrest be made and their BAC. (In any discussion session, "what if" situations are useful. WHAT IF you fail to arrest and the suspect drives two blocks and crashes into the police chief's car—and the chief thinks he is DUI?)

3. An in-house study project as to the reasons for DUI cases "lost" in court, and how best to react.
4. An in-house charting of judicial sentencing to identify traffic court judges who most frequently use probation, alcohol rehabilitation clinics, driver's training, and other out-of-prison devices when sentencing repeat DUI offenders, and how best to react if one judge is identified with inappropriate sentences. Officers can report sentencing details when reporting the disposition of a case. (Crime commissions in New York, Chicago, and New Orleans have used this charting for years as an effective and fair comparison of judicial sentencing).

Rest assured that the rank and file of any police agency will support zero tolerance DUI enforcement if it is fairly and honestly managed so that no one can brag about "beating" it.

Chapter 5

ENFORCEMENT

Traffic law enforcement is both punitive and educational. When a motorist is stopped by a police officer for violating one or more sections of the state's Vehicle Code, it is an unhappy event for that driver. If he or she is driving under the influence of alcohol and/or drugs, they should be aware of a possible arrest. If they have been driving recklessly or violating other "rules of the road," they can expect a citation and know that a "ticket" means a fine and possibly appearance in court—and is scored on their license file in the state Department of Motor Vehicles (DMV). Unhappy? Certainly, but on the threshold of learning.

Drivers who learn are less likely to cause accidents.

Drivers who never learn are chronic violators and participants in an increasing number of accidents. Soon, the driver's license of these "scofflaws" are suspended for a short period. If driving behavior is again disgraceful, revocation will leave them without a license to drive!

Driver Control

An effective driver control program requires interfacing activity by the police, courts, and the state DMV.

The objective of these three traffic-safety organizations is to gain a reduction in traffic accidents by identifying dangerous drivers and keeping them off the road, and by improving the safe driving habits of other drivers.

Citations are issued by police in lieu of arrest in the name of a local court with jurisdiction over violations of the state's vehicle code. Violations are described by name and section number of the Vehicle Code plus time, date, and location. The person named on this court paper (often termed a "summons") is directed to appear in such court at a specified date and time, usually 5–10 days after issuance, to answer to the violation of the Vehicle Code named and numbered in the citation. Also, these citations inform the driver that he or she can make this required "appearance" by mailing in a stated sum for the violation named, or appear in person for trial on a not guilty plea. (Mailing in the fine is a guilty plea.)

The violator usually has his or her case decided by a judge, particularly if it is changed to another denial of guilt such as a "no contest" plea. However, the violater may request a jury trial for many serious offenses, particularly cases of DUI.

The verdict, by judge or jury, is recorded in the court records along with the sentence. This disposition is reported to both the police department and the DMV.

In former years, police used this report of a court's action solely to note on their records the final disposition of a case. Likewise, DMV personnel made little use of this report, except for monthly and annual trends. Now, this report has utility. So has the DMV's massive file of all state residents licensed to drive a motor vehicle.

The Violator Point Count system was developed to achieve driver control by adding these reports of a driver's conviction of a violation of one or more sections of the state's vehicle code as a permanent notation on the driver's license record of each licensed driver. As part of the "point system," participation in accidents are noted in like fashion.

Points are "awarded" for serious moving violations and each accident, and too many points over specific periods can lead to suspension or revocation of a driver's license! (see Fig. 7).

This is the "whip" of the point system. Each driver knows when points are accumulating and that this means the loss of his or her license if not corrected. Prime motivation for change.

This method of assigning numerical values to convictions for violations of a vehicle code and being a participant in an accident is arbitrary, but is aligned with past performances of "problem" drivers and similar values in other states.

In California, legislators have enacted a violation point count as part of the state's Vehicle Code (Section 12810). Any conviction of the following violations of the Vehicle Code shall be given the value listed:

1. Failure to stop in the event of an accident ....2 points
2. DUI or DUI + injury ....2 "
3. Reckless driving ....2 "
4. DUI—minor under 21..2 "
5. Wrong-way driving...2 "
6. Speeding—over 100 mph ....2 "

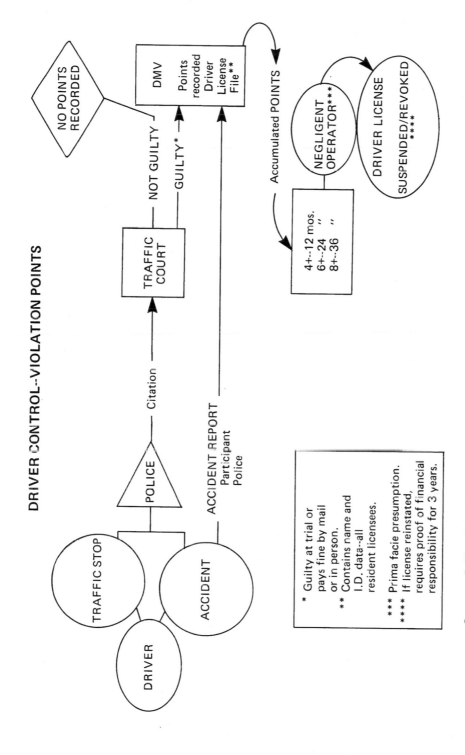

DRIVER CONTROL--VIOLATION POINTS

TRAFFIC STOP

DRIVER

ACCIDENT

POLICE

Citation

ACCIDENT REPORT
Participant
Police

TRAFFIC COURT

NOT GUILTY

GUILTY*

NO POINTS RECORDED

DMV

Points recorded

Driver License File**

Accumulated POINTS

NEGLIGENT OPERATOR***

DRIVER LICENSE SUSPENDED/REVOKED ****

4+--12 mos.
6+--24 "
8+--36 "

*   Guilty at trial or pays fine by mail or in person.
**   Contains name and I.D. data--all resident licensees.
*** Prima facie presumption.
**** If license reinstated, requires proof of financial responsibility for 3 years.

Source: California Vehicle Code Section 12810 et seq.

Figure 7. Citations for serious moving violations of California's Vehicle Code "earn" a driver from 1–2 points, and accidents account as 1 point if police describe driver as "responsible."

7. Knowingly driving—license suspended/revoked ....2 "
8. Any other violation—unsafe operation of vehicle ....1 "

Note. Participant in any accident if deemed responsible......................1 "

Limits are set for the maximum number of points in a set time period, and beyond these limits the driver is presumed to be an unsafe driver, and a prime candidate for license suspension or revocation.

Again, in California, these limits are:

1. Four or more points in twelve months
2. Six or more points in twenty-four months
3. Eight or or more points in thirty-six months.

Drivers exceeding these limits are *prima facie* presumed to be negligent drivers and their licenses may be suspended or revoked. However, due consideration will be given to persons who drive a great deal because of business or professional reasons. In addition, most DMVs send drivers a warning letter as they near the limit, and sometimes offer a safe-driving clinic to help in correcting their driving behavior.

Selective Enforcement

Selective enforcement is based on the prediction and prevention of future accidents from past experience. Selective enforcement is defined as enforcement proportional to traffic accidents with respect to time, place, and type of violation. Enforcement units are assigned to work in proportion to the traffic accident distribution by time and place, and the police effort is directed against accident-causing violations. Selective enforcement may result from the use of extensive studies and computer-based records systems, but it can also be based upon a manual study of accident records, an accident location spot map, or a responsive supervisor eager and ready to listen to the feedback from traffic officers working in the field.

Selective enforcement creates an impression of overwhelming force at accident locations. Police traffic enforcement patrols are assigned to such areas during the time of greatest accident incidence (day of week and time of day) and directed to enforce selected provisions of the vehicle code, usually moving violations which have been causing many of the accidents. Therefore, the force of selective enforcement is directed to reducing accidents by the on-view presence and the active patrol work of citing and arresting violators who drive in and through this area of high accident frequency during time periods in which most of the previous accidents have taken place. This is driver control through selective enforcement.

The contribution of selective enforcement to traffic control is that it is planned patrol work which creates an impression of police effectiveness in the minds of drivers using a certain area and, as a result, induces an unusual voluntary compliance with vehicle code regulations. Many police officers believe this public impression of extensive police operations can be enhanced by massive concentrations of police patrol units for selective enforcement in one area for a short period of time.

Enforcement Policy

The policy of enforcement must be set by the top administrator of the police unit. Too much fence-straddling in firmly establishing policy has fatal results on the effectiveness of an enforcement program. The officers on the street need to know just what is expected of them while at work.

The question of tolerance in traffic law enforcement is one requiring policy determination. Is the speed law going to be enforced at its legal limit? Behind the demand for realistic speed laws is the fact that tolerances may rest with the individual officer or at lower levels of supervisory command. The ideal situation is to have realistic speed laws and a policy of little or no tolerance.

What is the policy on speed pacing and measuring? Does the top executive demand legal or extra-legal procedure for the pacing and measurement of speeding violators? Or do frequent complaints by apprehended violators of eyeball clocks fail to stir an investigation of speed pacing practices? Police policy decisions should establish a middle ground for evidence gathering in speed cases.

Are rolling stops considered to be a fulfillment of the requirements of a stop sign, or must the motorist not only come to a full stop, but make that stop at the indicated line?

Has the top executive not only personally established the policy of not seeking help for friends involved in traffic law enforcement processes, but also established controls to prevent such intercession by lesser superior officers?

Has the top man or woman clearly established department policy on traffic law enforcement as not favoring any groups of individuals?

To be effective, policy must be clearly established, well communicated to all ranks, and firm and impartial. As a general rule police officers will work hard for an executive who clearly states what he or she wants and means it.

Enforcement Activity

The enforcement index has been described as a poor administrative tool and one likely to lead to charges of "quota." It is merely a rate expressing enforcement action (convictions for moving violations) for each fatal and personal injury accident. The enforcement action, when divided by the accidents, gives the enforcement index. An enforcement index of 20:1 is a balancing point: some areas and their accident problems may warrant more activity, and in others slightly less than 20:1 may be satisfactory.

Different sectors and varying times of the day are controlling factors in the individual activity of an officer. If enforcement activity needs enlarging, the best method is to spread traffic law enforcement throughout the entire uniform force. Administrative techniques, such as reducing time lost in court, traveling to and from post, and in the clerical work of citation preparation, will also mean more enforcement action.

Enforcement Techniques

Principal enforcement techniques generally fall into the following classifications:

1. Enforcement efforts by uniformed officers on intersection control duty or assigned to mobile units for general duty police patrol. The voluntary compliance aspect of this type of enforcement action exists only in the officer's presence.
2. Patrol and enforcement by traffic officers in plainly marked cars or on motorcycles. There is a high-level deterrent value, but again only in the presence of officers.
3. Enforcement at accident scenes for violations contributing to the accident. Usually effected by uniformed accident investigators, this enforcement has a value in accident prevention, but it is believed to be high because of its great selectivity of enforcement against the driver contributing to accident causation.
4. Patrol by uniformed officers in *unmarked* cars. This is a new

technique with a high voluntary compliance value that extends far beyond the presence of the officer.

5. Radar speed management by uniformed officers with plainly marked chase vehicles, but unmarked radar-screen cars. Radar has a high voluntary compliance ratio beyond the presence of the officer.

6. Speedometer operation by uniformed personnel. This form of speed management permits speed enforcement in areas not suited to pacing or not warranting radar speed management signing and enforcement. This is an effective deterrent beyond the presence of the uniformed officer, but hardened violators soon learn to look for the black tubes in the roadway. New clear plastic tubes are extending the psychological range of this device.

7. Air-ground speed control by an airborne patrol officer clocking violators with a stopwatch over previously marked stretches of highway with support from chase vehicles in the area. While aerial supervision is effective far beyond the presence of the uniformed officers, this technique is expensive and difficult to justify.

8. Safety checks or road blocks manned by uniformed officers in plainly marked vehicles. Preventive influence rests mainly in the field of persons operating without licenses or while their licenses are suspended, auto thieves, fugitives, and drunken drivers. It is effective but is presently lacking in public acceptance.

9. Rolling blocks by one or two police vehicles. Police vehicles set the pace for all following vehicles at the legal speed limit and physically prevent excessive speeds. It is effective mechanically, but public acceptance is limited.

Casual enforcement by general duty patrol officers has little effect on voluntary compliance, and while police action at accident scenes is very effective and truly selective, it is marked by the fact that it only reaches a small percentage of the total driver population. The most effective deterrents are police officers assigned to auto and motorcycle patrol, unmarked car patrol, and the psychological aids to enforcement in the field of speed management.

The effect of extending enforcement as a deterrent beyond the presence of the police officer can be achieved and should become an objective of police managers because it extends police coverage at little cost. It is used to extend the driver's belief in the omnipresence of the police.

There is proof that hazardous actions in violation of law lead to accidents. Drunken drivers are involved in a high percentage of accidents; speeding drivers not only become involved in accidents but also increase the normal severity potential of an accident by such driving; the individual who challenges another's right-of-way at a controlled intersection certainly rates attention for his accident potential. This does not necessarily mean that each of these violators will become involved in accidents, but more accidents occur as the result of such acts than occur when a driver is obeying all the laws for highway safety.

There is some proof that the sum of various enforcement techniques will reduce accidents. Possibly this conclusion may have to be tied in with the climate of an enforcement program; a rising trend of enforcement results in greater attention to education, engineering, and the enactment of improved legislation.

There is one thing about enforcement that is a certainty: Its impact is immediately felt by the driver population of a community. It is prompt and effective driver control. Education may take years for its influence to have any effect upon driving habits; engineering may take even longer to construct new and safety-engineered highways. Enforcement promptly deters violators. It is amazing how quickly a city's populations recognize slight changes in the quantity or quality of police traffic law enforcement.

There is also an emerging belief throughout the criminal justice establishment that the routine traffic stop has been one of law enforcement's most consistent ways to apprehend criminals. Routine traffic stops can easily end in discovering stolen cars with the driver behind the wheel, locating drugs on one or more occupants or in the car, finding all sorts of weapons, and identifying the driver as being wanted on an outstanding warrant. Arrests in such instances are meaningful.[*]

Protecting the Integrity of Police Action

The "fixing" of citations not only ruins the integrity of police enforcement, but also may influence police officers in their future relations with violators. A police officer who realizes that many of his or her traffic citations were fixed is certainly one with a lower threshold to bribery attempts than an officer who knows that no one else is going to profit

---

[*]Elaine Johnson, "Why Police Should Enforce Traffic Laws" *Traffic Safety,* Vol. 95 No. 1 (January/February 1995), 6–7.

because of police action originated by him or her in the service of a traffic summons. The officer secure in the knowledge that no one can tamper with his or her police action without being readily detected is also motivated to perform well on the job.

Written or telephone complaints of political interference should be investigated, not only to determine the truth or falsity of the allegations, but also to see whether or not the described conduct is similar to the known *modus operandi* of "influence" cases.

The modern methods of selecting and screening police officers put high caliber men and women on the street enforcing the traffic laws. Training enhances the basic honesty and integrity of these men and women. Interference can ruin such officers.

The auditing of police citations should be handled by a well-paid career city employee of the finance unit or the court system. In New York City, the Traffic Control Bureau of the Chief Magistrate's Office is responsible for New York's system of auditing police traffic action. Based upon computer procedures to save the expense of clerical personnel, this system unerringly indicates citations which have not been presented in court.

All citations are serially numbered; at the time of this numbering a duplicate record card is prepared. This record card is not removed from the file until the citation of the same number appears in a court complaint form. Therefore, individual police officers are directed to serve citations in numerical order. When a citation is served out of turn, the Traffic Control Bureau queries the police unit on what happened to the intervening summonses. This simple query is loaded and is the key to the audit system. The police officer must report whether or not the form was destroyed or mutilated and cite the attendant circumstances. If the police report states it was served and cites the circumstances of service, then the police direct a query to court personnel—what happened?

This "no-fix" traffic citation control cuts down on the number of cases that are lost. It insures optimum integrity for police action.

Chapter 6

TACTICS

The primary purpose of traffic law (Vehicle Code) enforcement is to encourage driver compliance with most of them. Whenever possible, the form of enforcement used should educate the violator. Becoming the subject of police enforcement action is a direct educational experience; drivers seeing police patrol cars on the highway is an indirect educational experience—but influential.

Patrol is the go-and-get-them tactic in most common use, auto or motorcycle. After observing the violation, officers on patrol go into the red-light-and-siren traffic stop and go to work.

Stopping the Traffic Violator

There are two basic decisions inherent in stopping traffic violators: (1) the decision that a violation has in fact been observed and (2) the appropriate level of enforcement action. There's been a great deal of careless talk about quotas in traffic enforcement patrol, and it is true there is likely to be administrative pressure from time to time for activity by officers on traffic patrol, but hard-working officers need never worry about satisfying any enforcement demands, and for this reason need never move to stop a violator in borderline cases or to take punitive action after stopping such motorists. An officer must be certain that the violation observed is complete in all of its essential elements and that the car he or she is about to stop is the offending vehicle observed. The basic ingredients for decision making as to appropriate enforcement action after stopping a violator are *fairness, impartiality,* and *uniformity.*

Enforcement action is usually limited to (1) a verbal or written warning, (2) a summons or citation requiring the offender's appearance in court, or (3) arresting the violator and transporting him to the area's designated police quarters for search, booking, and detention, pending release on bail or court arraignment. Experienced officers have found that enforcement action creates less emotional stress if they make this decision to

62

warn, cite, or arrest *before* the traffic stop is made. Of course, the contact during the stop may warrant greater action than initially contemplated; the driver may be drunk or operating a stolen vehicle, or the operator may be an emergency sick case or may be transporting an injured person in urgent need of medical attention.

Officer-violator communication is a problem. Early use of the siren and red light may contribute to a driver's decision to attempt flight. Reserving the use of siren and red light until the officer has closed on the offender's car is desirable but dangerous. Officers must be alert for motorists who will go into a panic braking and set up a situation likely to wreck both cars. Specific action in individual situations depends upon the driving ability of the police officer, his or her reaction time and intuitive level in evaluating the conduct of violating drivers during the short period of observation available for such analysis.

The stopping site should be of the officer's choosing. The objective is to get both vehicles out of the path of moving traffic and, at night, to find a well-lighted site. The shoulder of a road, if it is of sufficient width, is always a possible site. If a heavy truck is being stopped, the site should not be on a grade.

Experienced officers assigned to a new sector for the first time will usually attempt a circuit in search of suitable stopping places prior to any enforcement action. In congested areas, stops are usually made at available curbside spaces; officers should avoid double parking or the use of bus stops. If the violator does not stop at the place selected by the officer, it is necessary that an attempt be made to inform the violator to move his or her vehicle to the selected site, or if the violator has moved beyond this location, then to an alternate site of the officer's choosing.

Many police units require traffic officers to write the violator's license number on the "alarm" clipboard (usually left in the car when the officer exits for the violator contact) and to report by radio to the dispatcher the occasion of a traffic stop. Others require some meaningful details of the stop: location, description of car and occupants, and license (registration) number of the vehicle. A few police units ask their officers on patrol to delay contact until the license number of the vehicle has been checked against the current "wants." All police units ask officers to be alert for any suspicious movements, from changes in seating positions to the dropping of a shoulder, and to be watchful for violators with some of the characteristics of persons wanted on special "be alert for" alarms.

The position of the police car should be about eight to ten feet to the rear of the parked violator's car, with its center offset about three feet to the left side of the offender's vehicle. Day or night, the available warning and caution lights of the police car should be turned on and left in operation to warn approaching motorists. If the stop is at night, the headlights and spotlight of the police car should fully illuminate the offending vehicle and its occupants.

The approach on foot to a violator is always made in full recognition that the traffic stop may suddenly convert itself into a felony stop. A great many traffic stops are made along lonely and little-traveled portions of a highway system. This apparent isolation of the officer from immediate help by other officers, the lack of hostile witnesses, and the knowledge of the offender that his vehicle is readily available for prompt flight often develop mad-dog criminals out of previously run-of-the-mill offenders. The variable factor in this situation is the apparent and actual alertness of the officer. An apparent alertness might become a negative force in the offender's decision making; actual alertness prepares the officer for an unexpected attack.

Some police units drill their traffic officers in approach tactics for traffic stops to guard against any unusual situation distracting the officer from following standard procedure. In New York City, a motorcycle precinct commanding officer painted the positions of both the violator's car and the police vehicle in the approved traffic stop position on the floor of the police garage, and then painted footsteps to indicate the path of officers during the approach and contact.

Usually, the approach is from the driver's side of the police car to the same side of the violator's vehicle, with the officer's contact position being clear of any suddenly opened doors of the violator's vehicle and slightly to the rear of the front seat (this is an action position.) The driver is then ordered to stop the motor, if it is running. All the car's occupants can be watched. The driver is kept slightly off-balance in turning to make visual contact with the officer, and the officer can move into a defensive firing position if it is warranted.

Traffic conditions often force officers to adapt the above positions to the inboard or right side of both vehicles. The need for directing violators and possibly all the occupants of a vehicle to step out of the car also pulls the police officer out of a desirable position, but standard procedures offer the policeman some protection during this movement. If operating on the left side, the officer should direct the driver to step out and move to the front of the vehicle. Then, watching both the driver and any remaining occupants of the vehicle, the officer follows the driver and directs him to stand on the curb or sidewalk at the front right of his vehicle. If operating from the right, all occupants of the front seat are directed to step out and take positions along the right front of the violator's car. Remaining occupants, in either instance, are directed to exit one at a time from the right side of the car and line up alongside the others.

Officers driving a police vehicle are cautioned not to walk around the police car to get to its right side, but rather to slide across the front seat for this exit, to not walk between the cars, and to walk in front of the violator's car only once—to assure effective control of a suspect driver just removed from the car—and to make this transit as rapidly as possible if any remaining occupant of the car is in the front seat. Asking a suspect operator to remove his car keys from the ignition, or even to throw them out the window, is no guarantee of protection, as many cars can be started up promptly without a key.

The fact that no one item of this approach procedure can be slighted is highlighted by the killing of California Highway Patrolman Glen Carlson in 1963 on a mountain highway near Donner Lake. Carlson radioed for a license check and received notice that the car he planned to stop was stolen and its occupants were likely to be armed robbers. A nearby patrol car was dispatched to assist Carlson. However, the suspect car not only stopped at a site of its own choosing, but the killers also admitted to an exchange of seats in the car just before the stop. One of the occupants who had just changed seats from the rear to the front passenger seat, stepped out of the car just as the police car pulled to a stop in the rear of the suspect car. Carlson exited from the driver's side of the patrol car, ordered the passenger back into the car, and was shot across the rear deck of the suspect car. His assisting officer found Carlson dead on arrival about four minutes after the shooting!

Officer-Violator Contact

This is an interaction with the violator that should not be hurried. It can best be described as a sequence of taking the action decided upon before the stop, or which becomes necessary during the stop, and getting both cars safely back into the traffic stream without any loss of time.

Officer survival is again of primary importance. Many officers approach a traffic stop with considerable alertness, but relax during the contact.

This is a dangerous procedure. A good percentage of the officers who failed to survive a routine traffic stop were shot to death after the approach and during the officer-violator contact. Deputy Sheriff Bryce Patten of Ventura County (California) was shot to death in 1960 on a lonely highway after he had been handed the license of the suspect driver and the identification cards of two of the occupants.

Walking gait, facial expression, voice tone, and the phrasing of the initial comment of the police officer establish the frame of reference by which a violator reacts to this traffic law enforcement contact. The emotions of the driver of the car stopped are tautened by the sudden appearance of the police officer, by the knowledge he or she is being stopped for some wrongdoing, and by the interpretation of the ordinary rolling gait of some officers as indicating anger or aggression. This is also true of voice tone and the words used by the officer. Once the contact extends over thirty to forty seconds, this hypercritical attitude of the offender diminishes and his evaluative processes generally return to normal. However, sarcasm by the officer affects all violators adversely. When the suspect driver is a member of the minority group, any slighting forms of address or reference also create prompt resentment.

The attitude and language of the officer during this initial contact will indicate to the violator and the occupants of the stopped car whether or not the officer believes his traffic law enforcement work is meaningful. The indecisive, apologizing officer is an affront to the lifesaving aspects of vehicle code enforcement. The best approach is to immediately state the violation for which the offending driver has been stopped. In this initial statement the officer must communicate to the violator and the occupants of the car very definitely and firmly what was wrong and unlawful about the conduct for which the traffic stop was made. A caution to officers at this point in the contact is not to overexplain or be drawn into an argument. This can be avoided easily by a prompt request for the driver's license of the car's operator.

Patience is a necessity while the driver is seeking his license. The officer can appear busy and avoid the appearance of impatience by scanning the car's interior and any occupants (but avoiding being drawn into conversation with any occupant) and by asking the driver to take his license out of any wallet or plastic case in which it may be carried. This latter request avoids an initial rejection which does not help the officer-violator contact: the violator proffers the wallet, the officer rejects it and directs him or her to take the license out of the wallet or case. Officers should not reach into the violator's car for the license.

Alert to all movements by every occupant of the stopped car, the officer should check the expiration date of the driver's license and compare the stated physical description with the general appearance of the driver. Some officers ask the driver his date of birth, others his height or address. These questions assist in checking the data on the license, and they also are in accord with the basic principles of interviewing—asking a few commonplace questions which will relax the person being interviewed. An officer is fully justified in asking for further identification if there appears to be something wrong with the license and its data in comparison with the driver.

Where and how to stand when writing a warning or a ticket is complicated by light conditions and weather. Officers should not stand between cars or in front of the violator's car, nor should they lean upon or place their feet upon the violator's car. Officers should continue to watch the actions of the offender and any other occupants of the stopped car while preparing the citation, but many officers believe they can continue this surveillance and achieve better harmony in this contact by moving away from the violator's car toward the police car. Many police supervisors advise traffic officers that during this contact they must continue a conscious watch upon the passing traffic and to take a position in which they are not turned from this traffic.

Officers must work at writing the warning or citation, and at getting it completed (most of the routine entries of date, court appearance, court location, and officer's name can be filled in rapidly—and many police units permit advance preparation of such routine entries). When this is completed, the officer takes the same position in which he/she accepted the license from the driver—unless the operator had been directed or permitted to leave the vehicle—and hands the violator the written warning or ticket and returns the license.

In California and many other states, the violator is required to sign the citation. In these states, the officer must explain that the signature is not an admission of guilt in any way, but merely a promise to appear. The violator is advised to read the printed material just above the space indicated for his signature by a large "X." Most officers know this statement and read it aloud as a guide to the violator.

When the citation is accepted and signed by the violator (if required), the officer explains the need for responding to the specified court at or before the time indicated, whether or not the violation is one in which the violator may mail in a specified fine or if the violator must appear in person. However, the officer does not indicate in any way that the offender should plead guilty or not guilty, should or should not seek legal counsel, or comment on the amount of punishment common to violations for which the offender has been cited. During the entire contact, officers should avoid unnecessary conversation, but respond to reasonable queries.

If the offender signs the citation as required, the contact is over, and the officer should assist the violator to move his vehicle back into the traffic stream or, if traffic is not heavy, continue surveillance of the violator's car until it has departed the stopping site.

A citation is issued for a traffic violation in lieu of an arrest, and an arrest can always be properly made if the officer can justify not serving a citation. Usually, the problem is identity. In these infrequent cases the offender is cited at the police quarters after his identity has been established. Some jurisdictions will not permit nonresidents to be cited, and an arrest or some form of custody is required pending the posting of a bond for the court appearance of the defendant.

Immediately after the officer has informed the violator of being arrested, the officer will search the prisoner for weapons and evidence related to the offense. Such items and any contraband will be removed from the violator and retained by the officer.

The simple frisk (patting down) or the wall-search method may be used. In either case, officers must be alert for any movement or action by the violator which might be preliminary to an escape attempt or an assault upon the officer. The wall search may utilize the top, trunk lid, or engine hood of a car as a "wall." The principle of the wall search is that the offender is kept in an unbalanced position, being required to place his hands above his head on the wall and his feet well apart and as far from the base of the wall as possible. A supporting principle of this search is that the officer keeps one foot "hooked" in front of one of the prisoner's feet, ready to pull the prisoner's foot out from under him and bring him to the ground in the event of resistance. In either case, the officer does not (1) move in front of the prisoner, (2) place his weapon within easy reach of the prisoner, or (3) use more than one hand in searching the person of the prisoner.

Two offenders are not a great problem for one officer; he can search one offender and watch both of them with adequate effectiveness, but should use the wall-search method to put the offender waiting to be searched out of position for flight or a sudden attack on the officer.

When more than two prisoners are to be searched, officers must wait for back-up personnel. Police dispatchers routinely honor such requests. The assistance of fellow officers is a fine thing at any time; no officer should hesitate to ask for it.

Handcuffs are now standard equipment of police officers in the United States. Many police cars are equipped with two sets of handcuffs to supplement the officer's set. Many officers, particularly those working alone, handcuff prisoners prior to any kind of a search. Some officers dislike using handcuffs unless the crime charged is a felony or the offender has demonstrated some tendency to violence. In any event, the hands of the offender are usually cuffed together in the rear of his body. The cuffing of an offender's hands in front of his body permits the use of the joined hands and handcuffs as a weapon against the officer; an interlacing of the cuffs with an offender's belt is a makeshift and useless arrangement. Once cuffed, the offender or offenders should be placed in the back of the police car for transport to the place of booking and detention, unless other vehicles are provided for such transport.

A search of the offender is in order as incidental to a lawful arrest. Two 1973 U.S. Supreme Court decisions have established the doctrine that all custodial arrests are alike for purposes of search justification. In United States v. Robinson, 414 U.S. 218 (1973), the Court ruled that persons arrested for the offense of driving while their licenses have been revoked are not excepted from a police officer's general authority to search, incident to lawful custodial arrest, on the assumption that such persons are less likely to be possessed of dangerous weapons than those arrested for other crimes. In a companion case decided on the same day the Court's holding in Gustafson v. Florida, 414 U.S. 260 (1973) was that the search of a motor vehicle operator for driving without a valid operator's license in his possession was justified when the officer had probable cause to arrest the operator and lawfully effectuated the arrest and placed the operator in custody.

Some traffic patrol officers have developed two excellent search techniques in arrest cases. This is the searching of the area around the stopped cars for items which may have been dropped surreptitiously by the offender or flipped some distance away, and a thorough search of the police car before and after the prisoner's occupancy. Such searches may not only produce evidence, but offer the officer a possibility of establishing constructive possession by the violator.

When evidence is found during a search of the violator's person, his vehicle, the place of arrest, or of the car occupied by the prisoner while being transported after arrest, the police witness must be able to support the search as being incidental to the arrest or made with the express consent of the defendant. In *Mapp v. Ohio*, 376 U.S. 643 (1961), the United States Supreme Court ruled that a violation of the Fourth Amendment rule of reasonableness in searches is a denial of required due process (Fourteenth Amendment), and evidence obtained by searchers in violation of this constitutional requirement is inadmissible against the defendant.

If the evidence is related to a statement or admission of the defendant, it must be shown that he/she was not threatened in any way, made no promise that would invalidate a confession, nor was denied any rights guaranteed to all persons accused of crime and in police custody. All modern police officers realize the legal boundaries of police interrogation today: no physical or psychological threats, no promises which might induce an innocent man or woman to confess to a crime, and an adequate warning as to the right to silence and legal counsel during any custodial interrogation. Not only are police officers now required to warn persons in their custody, but they are also required to show by affirmative proof that the offender knowingly and intelligently waived his/her constitutional rights to silence (Fifth Amendment) and legal counsel (Sixth Amendment). In *Miranda v. Arizona*, 384 U.S. 436 (1966), the United States Supreme Court held that the prosecution must demonstrate the use of procedural safeguards effective to secure the privilege of any person against self-incrimination when police secure statements during custodial interrogation—questioning initiated by law enforcement officers after a person has been taken into custody or otherwise deprived of freedom of action in any significant way.

In DUI cases, however, officers should not confuse the admonishment as to the offender taking the chemical test to determine BAC with custodial interrogation. After an offender responds to questioning about his or her decision about taking the chemical test, Miranda is operable. It is world class double-talk to say: "You have a right to remain silent, but first you must answer this question." Officers in this situation should advise the suspect drunken driver that he or she has no right to have an attorney present before stating whether he or she will submit to this test, and in event of refusal, this refusal may be used against them in a court of law.

Traffic Patrol Techniques

There is an integration to good patrol, a mixing of basic procedures. Active patrol in which the traffic officer pursues and possibly paces the violator and takes enforcement action is mixed with off-street observation and passive or on-view patrol in which the traffic officer drives along with the traffic flow on a highway or parks on an intersecting highway in an open or on-view position. Methodical coverage of an assigned patrol area is mixed with specific coverage of hazardous areas or areas likely to be in need of police traffic enforcement patrol. Officers are assigned to specified and limited areas during designated hours, informed of violations causing accidents in these areas, and instructed to direct selective enforcement toward such violations.

Often an officer will find that off-street observation is not contributing to active patrol and abandons it in favor of a modified on-view patrol serving the dual purpose of being seen by motorists and making observations of driving behavior. An officer who merges with a traffic stream and drives from one end of his assigned sector to the other end is not being very innovative. The innovative officer may follow a group of cars, but when he has exhausted his observation of this vehicle group or when cars start to pile up behind the police car, he turns his vehicle around or exits from the highway and picks up another group of cars going in the same or another direction. While the innovative officer will not park in a "hole" or hidden off-street location, he will merge onto a highway from an access road when a large truck offers him the opportunity to do so unobserved by drivers of cars ahead who might be watching their rearview mirrors and speeding on the highway between access roads.

All patrol techniques should be oriented to observation. Officers who cannot secure activity in an assigned sector at some equality with other officers' activity on the same day of the week, at a like time, and under similar weather conditions, may be marginal employees for no other reason than poor capacity for observation.

An instructor in New York City's Police Academy often pleaded with patrol officers to develop the same enthusiasm for this work of observation as a "peeping Tom." He would recount several instances in his work as a detective in which he went up to these deviates and tapped them several times on the shoulder before he could draw their attention away from the subject of their "peeping." It was a weird but effective analogy: the recruit policemen associated patrol work with "looking."

Gathering Evidence

Evidence-gathering officers must remember the party in a criminal action claiming that a person is guilty of crime or wrongdoing or failed to exercise the requisite degree of care has the burden of proof on that issue. This rule of evidence calls for the prosecutor to initially produce evidence in support of the particular facts which constitute the violation with which the offender is charged. This is the classic *prima facie* case required in support of the probable cause upon which the police officer has based his citation or arrest.

Evidence is all the means used to prove or disprove a fact in issue. Proof is the result or effect of evidence. In determining the credibility of a witness, courts or juries may consider any matter that has any tendency in reason to prove or disprove the truthfulness of the testimony of such person. It may include, but is not limited to: (1) the demeanor of the witness while testifying, (2) the character of the testimony, (3) the opportunity of a witness for perception and the capacity of a witness for recollection, (4) the opportunity of a witness to discover evidence and the capacity to protect its integrity, (5) the existence or nonexistence of any fact testified to by the witness, (6) the existence or nonexistence of a bias, interest, or other motive, (7) a prior statement that is consistent or inconsistent with the witness' testimony, (8) the witness' attitude toward the action, and (9) the admission of untruthfulness.*

Excellent evidence for the trial of an offender is physical evidence which *transfers* from crime scene to suspect, suspect to scene, victim to suspect, and suspect to victim. The police officer must be prepared to testify to his finding of items of physical evidence and of a chain of possession indicating the character of the evidence has been maintained since its finding, despite laboratory examination by chemical, spectrographic, or other analysis. Police witnesses, when shown such evidence, must be in a position to say they recognize it as the item found by them (describing *where, how,* and *when*) and the source of recognition (general

---

*Paul B. Weston and Kenneth M. Wells, *The Administration of Justice,* 2nd Ed. Englewood Cliffs, Prentice-Hall, 1973), pp. 210–211.

appearance of the item of evidence and the officer's act at the time of its finding of scratching upon the item his initials or sealing it within a container and initialing the container). This is necessarily followed by showing that the evidence was placed in an evidence locker or "signed in" for safekeeping and possibly laboratory examination in accordance with the ordinary course of business as required by local police rules and regulations. Otherwise such evidence will never be legally significant, as its credibility is in question.

Criminals on the Highway

In 1988, the Louisiana State Police reported a new in-service school with instructional material designed to enhance the ability of their troopers to detect, identify, and apprehend criminals traveling the state's highways. Emphasis was on recognition of the vehicles and conduct of people transporting drugs, stolen property, firearms, or missing and exploited children.* Today, this instruction is almost universal, and extended curriculums cover youth and the violent crimes of children and young adults.

Criminals use the highways. They do not overtly disobey vehicle code regulations; there is a strong suspicion they are our most "law-abiding" motorists when they have cause to avoid police inspection of any kind. Many criminals also sell stolen merchandise along highways. Some highway business establishments are suspicious premises because of criminal operations or patronage by members of the underworld. A few of the premises along highways concerned with the repairing, towing, and wrecking of vehicles may harbor unlawful activity. If an officer on traffic patrol cannot develop probable cause for a summary arrest, it is effective police work to report upward the circumstances causing an alert and observant traffic officer to suspect criminal operations.

---

*W. McCormick, "Criminal Patrol Techniques", *FBI Law Enforcement Bulletin*, Vol. 57, No. 1 (January 1988), pp. 119–22.

Chapter 7

SPEED MANAGEMENT

S peed management is a crucial factor in highway safety. The philosophy underlying the enforcement of maximum speed laws is that compliance with reasonable regulations will contribute to the safe and efficient movement of vehicle traffic on a street and highway system.

Unfortunately, there has been an air of uncertainty about the 55 mph National Maximum Speed Limit (55 mph NMSL). This nationwide edict as to the speed of motor vehicles was initially an energy (gasoline) conservation measure. It was soon identified as a lifesaving law in that there were over nine thousand (9,353) fewer fatalities from vehicle accidents in the first year the law was in effect. Supporters of the 55 mph NMSL claimed drivers were slowing down and this speed reduction was saving lives. The uncertainty arises because a fair proportion of traffic experts and members of the general public believe a reduction in vehicle use is responsible for this life saving aspect of the 55 mph NMSL. People just do not drive as much as they formerly did. In addition, critics of the 55 mph NMSL say the reality is that there is no slow down; the 55 mph regulation is marked by its violation rather than its compliance.

In truth, lifesaving on the highways since 1974, the year in which the 55 mph NMSL legislation became law, is probably a combination of reduced speed, fewer miles driven, and altered driving habits, such as driving at desired speeds (above 55 mph) only under ideal traffic, roadway, and weather conditions.[*]

Historically, the concept of state's rights placed responsibility upon state governments for enacting legislation designating behavior that is criminal as opposed to noncriminal behavior, and since the advent of the automobile it has been the responsibility of state governments to enact legislation concerning automobiles and their safe operation. There has

---

[*]Institute of Transportation Engineers, Metropolitan Section of New York and New Jersey, Subcommittee on 55 mph Speed, "Implications of the Mandatory 55 mph National Speed Limit," *Traffic Engineering* (February 1977), pp. 21–24.

been some uniformity in the provisions of these state vehicle codes, but the attempts several years ago to establish total uniformity in accordance with a suggested Uniform Vehicle Code was unsuccessful. (Within certain limitations, local governments within each state have authority to enact local laws for the control of vehicle and pedestrian traffic.)

In the state of Nevada, legislators never established a maximum speed law on rural highways, allowing motorists to set their own speed limit, depending upon road conditions. Other states in the West, with considerable mileage between urban areas, are also oriented to the reality of motorists driving at high speeds between urban areas. California highways are illustrative of this orientation. In constructing their extensive freeway system, California engineers designed major portions of these roads to handle vehicles traveling at 70 mph with safety. This is also true of the United States Interstate System. Portions of this limited-access highway system were similarly engineered, and speeds such as 70 mph allowed when not in conflict with state maximum speed laws.

The initial reaction of state legislators was to accept the 55 mph National Maximum Speed Limit as an energy conservation measure that would be enforced in accordance with the state's official attitude toward a maximum speed. In many states this meant that only those motorists responding to the energy conservation aspects of the 55 mph speed law obeyed it during the first few months of 1974. However, when state and local police began to enforce the 55 mph speed limit, some legislators suggested curtailing funds for police budgets. In some areas, judges were critical of police enforcement and fined violators only a few dollars or dismissed the charges without punitive action, unless there was some proof that the speed was really excessive for the conditions at the time of the violation.

This attitude and allegations of little or no police enforcement pressure led to legislation requiring the governor of each state to certify annually to the Secretary of Transportation that the 55 mph speed limit on all public highways is being enforced. To insure adequate enforcement of the 55 mph NMSL within each state, this legislative provision also empowers the Secretary of Transportation to withhold approval of federal aid highway construction projects in any state failing to certify enforcement of the 55 mph NMSL.

This legislative edict means that millions of dollars in federal highway construction funds can be withheld from states in which the police and courts do not enforce the 55 mph NMSL.

Because some of the annual certifications required of each state were considered inadequate, legislation for this certification was adopted and became effective on September 9, 1975.

This provision requires each state to report and certify the results of an annual audit of the number of citations issued for violation of the 55 mph speed limit, and a monitoring of highway traffic to determine the 85th percentile and other speeds above 55 mph.

It is interesting to note that this new amendment requires each state to report on the "85th percentile speed" discovered as a result of their program of monitoring motorists' speeds on the state's streets and highways. At one time, traffic engineers and state legislators used the 85th percentile speed as a guide to enactment of maximum speed laws. This was a standard found useful in prior years because any speed used by 85 percent of the motorists using a particular highway was considered a realistic speed oriented to the physical characteristics of the highway and the comfort of the motorist and was generally considered a safe speed.

Other data required of states by this legislative amendment is data gathered from the state's speed monitoring program as to the percent of motorists exceeding 55, 60, and 65 mph. While this data will indicate the observance rate in the state in regard to the 55 mph NMSL, unlike the 85th percentile speed, this data does not indicate the "desired" speed at which the great majority of motorists generally operate.

Conflict between the 55 mph NMSL and the desired speeds of most motorists may be the reason federal authorities now emphasize the lifesaving feature of the 55 mph NMSL. There appears to be some recognition of the fact the contribution to energy conservation is not meaningful to most motorists, but any program saving lives on the highway can be meaningful.

A life-saving 55 mph speed limit is also difficult to revoke. On several occasions, legislation has been introduced in Congress to return to the states their right to write their own laws, but without success. Our national legislators may now be tuned in to the professional beliefs of traffic and highway experts that higher speeds can be safe and more convenient—and more likely to be obeyed.

In a democracy, public acceptance of newly enacted laws generally results from the basic merit of the legislation, and police enforcement is necessary only for the relatively small percentage of the public that disobey such laws. Unfortunately, the 55 mph NMSL was not in response to public pressure for a limitation of vehicle speeds. This law was enacted during an energy crisis to conserve gasoline. Many motorists have mixed emotions regarding the politics associated with energy and its conservation in the United States and have little concern for the few pennies that might be saved by the acceptance of lower speeds that consume less gasoline. As a result, the police of the United States are confronted with a basic problem: enforcement of an unpopular law.

In 1995, the U.S. Senate voted to revoke the national 55 mph limit (65 mph on rural highways) for passenger cars but decided to keep the limit for heavy trucks and buses. State's-rights representatives appear to assure a favorable vote in the House. A year or two under different mph speed limits in various states and statisticians should have informative data on the impact of changes.

Police Speed Management Techniques

Most state and local police agencies operate a basic speed management program in areas in which speed has been identified as a prime cause of accidents and/or areas in which speed monitoring has revealed average speeds in excess of the 55 mph NMSL. Basic to these programs is patrol by traffic officers, during which the officers observe the traffic flow on a highway and identify suspect speeding vehicles, pursue and pace such vehicles, and take enforcement action when the suspect vehicle is "clocked" at speeds above the 55 mph maximum.

During the years in which these basic programs were developed, police administrators were responsive to the negative public reactions to behind-the-billboard tactics and so-called "speed traps." As a result, these basic programs have a policy of visible enforcement and a pacing or clocking of speeding vehicles.

The importance of speed management in saving lives on the nation's highways, however, led to the adoption of radar devices to measure the speed of moving vehicles. Radar is an electronic device now available from numerous manufacturers. It accurately measures the speed of vehicles within its "zone of influence." It is usually placed in a position, in or out of a police vehicle, alongside the highway to monitor approaching cars. Since the zone of influence of the radar extends for a considerable distance, the speed of approaching vehicles is measured before the drivers know it. Cars violating the speed limit are signaled to stop by a uniformed officer, who also serves the violator with a citation for speeding. Drivers of cars ignoring the "wave down" are pursued by a "chase" car which is usually positioned further down the highway. When apprehended, additional appropriate action is taken against these violators for failing to stop at the direction of an officer.

Expert witnesses have testified in various courts across the country as to the mechanics of these devices, and most courts now accept radar as an accurate and dependable device for measuring the speed of vehicles.

Police traffic officers and the managers of police agencies often favor radar devices over the pacing-and-clocking method because radar measurement lessens the hazard to officers. Any pacing or clocking of speeding vehicles is hazardous duty, and the higher the violator's speed the greater the chance for officers becoming involved in accidents with other vehicles in the traffic stream. In speed management with radar, the only vehicles pursued are vehicles whose drivers refuse to obey instructions to stop by the officer tending the radar device.

Police managers also favor radar devices because radar speed measurement brings an additional element of supervision to speed management. The record made by the radar device as speed is measured identifies every vehicle exceeding the speed limit, so officers have no opportunity to favor any motorist by not taking appropriate enforcement action. The policy of most police agencies is to require officers operating radar devices to serve citations for each excessive speed violation recorded. The only exceptions are test runs by police vehicles to check the accuracy of the radar device, or the passage of authorized emergency vehicles, and officers are required to make detailed note of these circumstances on the radar record.

Police managers may also favor radar because this device has a high "production" record. In comparison with pacing-and-clocking, more citations for speeding can be served by fewer officers in less time.

Public reaction to radar ranges from acceptance to rejection. Acceptance is indicated by violators' comments to officers tending radar devices that they knew they were speeding, and by the high percentage of guilty pleas in response to citations resulting from radar measurement of speed.

Rejection appears to be a public reaction to radar devices as a modern-age speed trap and nonvisible enforcement. The first group rejecting this technique is the drivers who continually scan their rear view mirrors for signs of police pacing-and-clocking and dislike radar devices because the police presence cannot be detected in such fashion. The existence of another, and possibly even larger, group of motorists is revealed by the popularity of radar detection devices and Citizen Band (CB) radios. In the first instance, motorists use an electronic countermeasure to notify them by some audio signal that they are approaching the zone of influence of a police radar device. CB radios may be popular for many reasons, but one of the factors in the wide use of these transmitter-receivers is warnings about police radar activity. This communication is a personal notification between CBers about the locations of police tending radar devices. Since many of these be-aware-and-slow-down messages are sent by drivers who were not stopped at the radar installation, as they were not at the time exceeding the speed limit, it is safe to assume that such drivers reject the concept of radar speed management. While the legality of these two warning methods may be questioned, they do serve in some degree as a countermeasure to radar speed management.

Except for California, where public pressure upon state legislators has forbidden the use of radar to the California Highway Patrol, more and more state police and statewide traffic patrols are adopting radar for speed management. Georgia, Maryland, New York, Oregon, Washington, and Massachusetts are among the states that have adopted radar for speed management. The Washington State Patrol use mobile radar in their patrol cars. This is a form of radar device that measures the speed of oncoming vehicles while the police car is in motion. The Massachusetts State Police describe radar as being an innovative and productive technique used by their "55 Teams." These are teams of six men charged with speed management, who not only use radar but may also use it in tandem—placed two or three miles apart to intercept speeders.

Photo Radar is a joinder of a radar "gun" and a camera. Together, any vehicle exceeding the speed limit triggers the mechanism and the speed is recorded and displayed, the front and rear of the car (including registration plates) and the driver are photographed. The registered owner of the offending vehicle is notified and asked to pay a specified fine. It is self-operating, but requires personnel to service its operation.[*]

Antispeeder Enforcement and Education

As a threshold to educating the general public about speeders, the police should provide news media with data on collisions caused by speeding drivers. The means must equate with availability on the local

---

[*]Kevin M. Morrison, *Speed Measurement in Traffic Law Enforcement—From Radar to Laser* (Jacksonville, Florida, University of North Florida, Institute of Police Technology and Management, 1995), pp. 40–42.

scene. Press releases and TV "spots" by the chief or other leading officers are a place of beginning.

The public should be made aware that speed does kill and worsens injuries in vehicle collisions. Speed has justly been blamed for about a quarter of all fatal and disabling-injury accidents. These violaters knowingly and wilfully step on the gas, viewing speed limits as guidelines for driving rather than laws, and getting away with speeding akin to winning some one-on-one sporting event.* Police know the facts about these people and can speak from experience. Driving 100 mph down a lonely super highway may be "fun"—until the speeder rear-ends a slow-moving vehicle filled with high school students. Driving 50 mph through a school zone is not obscene—until the speeding driver hits and kills a school crossing guard.

Mothers Against Drunk Driving (MADD) have labored long and hard to rid our roads of drunk drivers and have been successful. Founded by a mother grieving the death of her daughter by a DUI repeater, they have raised the social stigma of being a drunk driver from zero to measurable levels. Hopefully—and soon—a father grieving over the loss of a child to a speeding driver totaling a car in a head-on collision may found a Fathers Against Speeding Drivers. (A grieving dad in California, angry because his daughter was killed by an ex-convict on parole, led a successful fight for 3-strike legislation—banning parole for 3-time felons.)

An aware public can do great things! A public full of motorists has a need to know that speeders are not the "good guys" of the highway. For instance: A deputy sheriff attempted to stop a driver for speeding at about 1:00 A.M. The driver turned off the headlights of his late-model Honda and took off. After a 13-mile chase at speeds topping 100 mph, the deputy stopped the fleeing driver, and—expecting the driver to flee on foot—got out of his patrol car, and watched as the speeder suddenly started up his car, turned, and tried to run down the deputy! A "good guy"? No!"

As many people as possible must be made aware of the hazards of speeding beyond legal limits and what it means for them and theirs—and others.

Of course, many drivers will reject any attempt to slow down. A fair percentage of these men and women will be detected by officers on the

*David Murray, "Let's Get Serious About Speeding, *Traffic Safety* (January/February 1994), Vol. 94, No. 1, pp. 12–15.

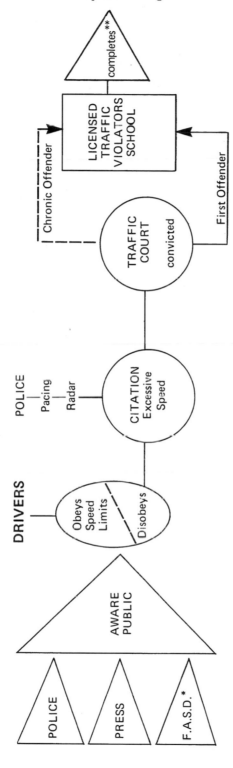

Figure 8. An aware public, police, and local judiciary combine to influence and educate drivers to obey limits on speeding.

highway "clocking" suspect violators. If driving at excessive speed, violators will be issued citations ordering them to appear in traffic court. Violators pleading guilty or found guilty after trial will be sentenced to attendance at a traffic violators school—usually as a condition of probation. This is usually an "either or" proposal and most convicted offenders are happy to attend school—rather than receive other punishment.

In most jurisdictions, these schools are licensed by the Department of Motor Vehicles, operate under strict rules as to faculty and curriculum, and have an adjunct status with the local traffic court—reporting to the sentencing judge "students" who successfully complete a prescribed course or fail to do so. Students failing are resentenced (see Fig. 8).

The theme of this antispeeding program is education and retraining. Speed management by police does not stand alone, unsupported by public opinion or any effort to retrain convicted speeders. This cooperative effort brings together the major agents concerned with reducing traffic accidents and their severity.

Chapter 8

OFFICER SURVIVAL

Police officers in the United States are being attacked with an appalling frequency during routine stops of motorists on our streets and highways. These are murder-in-progress attacks. Attackers are intent on getting away from the officer—to escape. They act on the slightest cue from the victim-officer that they can do it and escape, and the only defense is the target officer's reaction and action!

There are many problems that suddenly arise when the so-called routine stop of a traffic violator turns into an attack on the officer making the stop. What is the signal of danger? What is the position of an officer who surrenders his service revolver in these situations? What if the violator takes a fellow officer as a hostage? Should traffic officers approach traffic stops with unholstered guns?

No one has isolated any act of a violator that could be classed as an early warning signal. It has been possible to detail overt acts suggesting the imminence of an assault. However, despite a delineation of overt warning signs, many officers fail to observe them and react in self-defense, or else refuse to accept an observed warning sign as a cue to immediate defense action and react too late for effective defense.

It may be that the officer is surprised after years of routine stops and refuses to accept the warning in the hope of some last-minute magic proving that his first impression was wrong, that this could not be happening in reality. One officer, with more than one overt warning given him by a violator, was found dead with his revolver holstered and his shotgun on the ground. The shotgun had not been fired, nor did it have a shell in its chamber!

Lastly, officers making traffic stops must remember that no fast draw in the world equals a keen and alert mind and the development of an intuitive reaction to danger. Officer survival may depend on the ability of individual officers to pull together apparently meaningless clues and get the police handgun out of its holster. It may be nothing more than a dropped shoulder during an apparently normal pacing of a speeding violator, a slight change in the silhouette of a driver after rounding a curve during a lengthy pursuit, a little unusual tenseness apparent in the violator's stopping of his car or an overly friendly reception upon the approach of the officer.

Routine Stops

Police academy indoctrination establishing the police officer as the "nice guy" of officer-violator contacts, years of routine stops without even a threat of armed resistance, and public relations-oriented commanding officers function together to create a sense of well-being about routine stops of vehicles by police officers for violations of the vehicle code. It is a *de facto* conspiracy of two or more circumstances to place public relations as the primary aspect of traffic violator stops.

A more realistic frame of reference would array the various aspects of traffic violator stops in this order:

1. Traffic violator may be a killer.
2. Law enforcement (primary rationale for stop).
3. Public relations.

Using this frame of reference, a police officer would always be *on guard*, in a position of readiness to *take command* of the officer-violator stop. This does not mean that the officer's service revolver, or other assigned firearm, will be used as an offensive weapon, but that the officer will display the weapon in a position of readiness whenever the driver or other occupant of a stopped car behaves in a manner the officer believes to be threatening to his/her personal safety. This is the moment of *taking command.*

The officer acts to stop the movement of driver and occupants, if any, to develop measures of safety. Now, the officer no longer makes requests as in a normal traffic stop; he/she gives *orders.* All of the commands should be given in a clear and steady voice above the volume of normal conversation: *loud and clear.* The content of the officer's orders should be short and simple, and progressive. For instance, assume the suspects (driver and occupants) are to be removed from the driver's side of their car. The commands given should follow in this order:

1. Don't turn around. Keep looking straight ahead.
2. Driver! Put your hands on the top of the steering wheel—both hands.

3. You, in the front seat, put your hands on the windshield—palms against the glass.
4. You, in the rear seat, put your hands on the back of the front seat—palms up.
5. All of you keep looking straight ahead.
6. Nobody move until I tell you to move.

In threatening situations in which a violator, and possibly occupants of the vehicle, confronts a police officer on the highway, the major threat to the officer is the fast-breaking characteristics of the situation. No one, in book or classroom, can adequately describe what will happen nor how fast it does happen. It is for this reason that the words "taking command" are so very appropriate, as this phrase implies equally rapid action by the officer to halt and *hold* the fast-breaking threat to his/her personal safety.

Officers have been shot long after a threatening situation first became evident because they relaxed and the violator was able to overcome them. The following case illustrates not only taking command but also holding command—never relinquishing it until all threat to the officer has been resolved.

State Police Officer Blue had been briefed by his area commander at 0630 hours, at the beginning of his tour of duty, to be on the alert to detect a 1956 black Volkswagen®, with the license plate AID696. The vehicle had been identified as the getaway car in a series of armed robberies, the latest a few hours before the tour started. The car's occupants and suspects were two white male juveniles (WMJ) about seventeen to twenty years of age and a white female juvenile (WFJ) of about sixteen to seventeen years of age.

Officer Blue was on routine highway patrol at approximately 0735 hours when he noted a vehicle matching the description of the "wanted" vehicle passing him in the opposite direction. He could not see the license plate. To confirm that this was the correct vehicle, he made a U-turn and proceeded after the vehicle. As the Volkswagen approached the Edenvale exit, it abruptly turned off and went southward on Edenvale, and at this time Blue lost sight of the vehicle for approximately seven seconds. (He had not notified his area office by radio as there are many black Volkswagens, so he wanted to check the vehicle closer before calling in.) As he made the left turn on Edenvale to go south, Blue immediately noted the Volkswagen stopped on the shoulder approximately *sixty yards* south of Grant Road. He was on top of the Volkswagen without being able to use the radio and immediately noted two things: (1) the license number was AID696 and (2) the occupants in the vehicle were two WMJs and one WFJ, and they were changing positions in the car and making many furtive movements!

Blue stopped his vehicle behind the Volkswagen off-center to the left and approximately *sixty feet* north of its position. The occupants seemed aware of his presence, and rather than have them get out of their vehicle and come back on both sides of the patrol vehicle, Blue stepped out of his vehicle with the outside speaker on his arm and with the shotgun (inserting a round into the chamber of the shotgun as he exited). Using the patrol vehicle as protection, he advised the suspects over the P.A. system (outside microphone/speaker) that it was the State Police, and for all to place their hands on the ceiling of the Volkswagen where he could see their arms. They did. He then carefully called his dispatcher and asked for backup assistance and advised what he had. Blue then instructed the driver to slowly take the keys out of the ignition and throw them out the left front (LF) window. He then directed him to place his hands out of the LF window, open the door from the outside, and get out of the vehicle, facing toward him, keeping his hands over his head. The driver was then ordered to kneel, cross his feet and put his hands over his head while facing away from the patrol vehicle. The other passengers were ordered out in a similar manner, and all complied. (It should be noted that during the entire time period the suspects were kept within the shotgun "pattern," and officer Blue never moved from the protection of the patrol vehicle. He *held* command of the situation.)

State police officer Dallas arrived at the scene and, using his shotgun, moved up on the right of the Volkswagen out of officer Blue's line of fire and checked for further occupants, with negative results. State police officer Austin and Sergeant Houston then arrived. This location on Edenvale is approximately one block away from Edenvale High School, and the principal, on his way to work, stopped and offered assistance. At this time officer Blue put his shotgun away and, gathering three sets of handcuffs, advanced and handcuffed the three suspects. Officers Dallas and Austin each took a male suspect and searched them for weapons with negative results. Sergeant Houston took custody of the female suspect with the school principal watching.

At this time Blue was called back to the radio and, as he reached for the microphone, Sergeant Houston called for him to come back to his location; Blue did this immediately. The female suspect was wearing a blouse, jacket, slacks, and cowboy boots; while Sergeant Houston had been conducting a pat-down search, he had noted a bulge in the crotch area of her slacks, which resembled a pistol. With officer Blue and the principal watching, Sergeant Houston reached into the crotch area of her capris and removed a fully loaded .22 caliber pistol. (A complete search of the vehicle later turned up an additional thirty-five rounds of .22 ammunition.)

An important aspect of this stop is that the situation forced Officer Blue to take action without a backup unit present; his complete control of the situation brought an otherwise not so routine stop to a proper conclusion. The concealed .22 caliber pistol was an ongoing threat to officer survival *throughout* this stop until its disclosure.

In review, after proof that the three juveniles were involved in no less than six recent armed robberies, it is apparent that they attempted to trap the police officer. The suspects' selection of the site for stopping and their apparent willingness to comply with instructions might have allowed them to overcome a careless police officer and make their escape.

A routine stop is not over until the officer and the violator separate, and the motorist drives off down the highway. Officers must maintain continuous command control until this ending of the stop. Dispatchers panic when an officer who had just talked to them breaks off a transmission and then doesn't respond to frantic attempts to contact him.

When the last few minutes of a routine stop turn sour, the local dispatcher usually has some knowledge of the stop, a warrant or a license check—often, the location as well. Unfortunately, all that officers find after rushing to the scene is a dead or seriously wounded officer.

In one recent case on the East Coast, investigators did develop just about what happened during the closing moments of one routine stop. Piecing together the dispatcher's conversation and the story of a passing motorist, investigators reconstructed the scene: At 2040 hours a 10-year veteran trooper named Long reported stopping a 1970 or '71 Oldsmobile on U.S. 75 just north of Shell Road. His next contact was a query to the dispatcher as to the registration number of the plate on the Olds. A few minutes later, when she had a "no wants" result, she called Long. No response. No response. Alert, she transmitted an "assist trooper" message for U.S. 75 and Shell Road. The passing motorist was found by the first trooper at the scene, he was talking to the dispatcher over Long's radio and screaming for an ambulance. Later, he told investigators he had been just about to pass the police car when he saw a small man in a dark shirt walk up to the window of the police car and lean in. He added that he heard two quick shots just as he slowed down to pass the patrol car. He sped past until he could find a level spot on the medium to make a U turn and raced back to the scene.

Long, shot twice in the head, never spoke. He was declared DOA on arrival at a nearby hospital. His assailant was captured about twenty minutes later, speeding down U.S. 75! This suspect stone-walled questioners all day, and hung himself from his cell bars that night.

The last best guess of investigators was that Long was dissatisfied with the driver's i.d., had returned to his car to query the dispatcher, and was reaching for his microphone when he was shot.

Surrender Under Threat

It is no longer a routine stop when an officer hears the words, "Give me your gun, motherfucker!". Suddenly, the driver is in charge, pointing his or her gun at the officer or holding it to the head of a fellow officer. The demand is repeated once more—shouted—screamed. It is a tense moment. What to do?

Basically, there are three immediate-action options: talk, shoot, or disarm the guy or gal with the gun.*

Talking an armed suspect "down" may be possible. The theme should play to knowledge that most cop-killers are caught, convicted, often earn a death sentence, and police never give up looking for cop-killers.

Shoot it out is a decision that may bring devastating fire before a weapon can even be drawn from its holster. On the other hand, the element of surprise may gain an officer the time necessary to be successful.

Disarming is possible only if an officer can reach the weapon aimed at him or her—and knows how to do it. It is not easy, but can be a very meaningful response.

A delayed-action option is to surrender and wait for an opportunity to regain control of the situation. Some officers arm themselves with a "back-up" gun, wearing it on the belt behind a handcuff case or in a boot

---

*Paul B. Weston, *Combat Shooting for Police*, Springfield, IL, Charles C Thomas, 1960, pp. 38–39.

or ankle holster. Firearms manufacturers now offer small, heavy-caliber automatic pistols designed as contingency weapons.

Any hostage seized and used by an armed criminal in defense against an armed officer creates a special problem. Again, only the officer faced with this problem can answer as to the best action. Some officers who work together quite frequently work out signals helpful to planned resistance.

Ambush Attacks on Police Officers

An ambush attack is described as a sudden fast-breaking event in which the armed assailant or assailants surprise the police officer victim. It is marked by a lack of provocation in that it was not provoked in any way by the behavior of the target officer. The victim officer is a symbol against which the assailant acts out antisocial drives and/or serious emotional problems. The victim officer may be shot at from long range from a concealed position (sniping) or directly attacked at close range without any attempt at concealment. One ambush began with an anonymous telephone call reporting an accident. There was no accident at the location given, but the officers were fired upon shortly after their arrival. Other officers have been attacked while they were conducting traffic stops, the ambushers acting out the role of an ordinary citizen and simply walking up to the unsuspecting officer.

Since ambushers may have superior firepower as they are frequently armed with semiautomatic and large caliber weapons, ambushed officers should first seek cover before returning an assailant's fire. Police vehicles offer cover and some protection from armed attack. Sidewalk mail boxes, hydrants, the corners of buildings, and light standards offer similar cover and protection in urban areas; stone walls, large rocks, and ditches offer a similar safe refuge in rural areas. In any location, an officer should find some object that will at least conceal him or her from an ambusher. The exigencies of police duty now demand a new watchfulness from police officers—as an officer survival technique. This is a second sense awareness of the physical characteristics of a location so that an officer can promptly seek cover when the unexpected does happen.

The best defense against any ambush attack is an individual's alertness prior to the event. There are "early warnings" in many ambushes. A perceptive and watchful officer will pick up danger signals and will heed them, taking prompt action to neutralize the surprise aspect of an ambush.*

An officer may stop any assault if he or she has their weapon in their hand, out of the holster, and ready to shoot: magazine in place, cartridge (live round) in firing position in chamber, safety in OFF position. (Revolvers need only to be loaded (5–6 rounds in chamber) as they do not have a "safety" and can be fired double action.)

In this connection, there is some sensitivity among police officers about the directive of many public relations-oriented police administrators restricting the circumstances under which an officer may draw his weapon in traffic stops. Officers in the street believe they are in a better position to make this vital decision than desk-bound executives. Pending the relaxing of these restrictions, most men and women have formed the reasonable belief that it is far better to be a live police officer being disciplined for an infraction of local rules than it is to be a dead or dying officer found on the highway with his revolver in his holster.

Over a quarter century ago, two Los Angeles detectives stopped a car with a driver and one occupant. Probable cause for the stop was a dirty license plate; actually they thought the car was "suspicious" and its occupants should be "checked out." Neither detective expected resistance; one of the suspects exited the car, walked casually behind one of the detectives, drew a loaded pistol from the waistband of his trousers and shoved it into the detective's back. From this position he told the other detective to surrender his weapon or his partner would be shot. The surrender was made, the suspect with the gun took the "hostage" detective's gun from its holster, herded the two of them into the "suspicious" car, waved his crime partner in, and took off. About two hours later, one detective was shot dead in an onion field outside Los Angeles, his partner escaped being killed by fleeing in the early-morning darkness.†

Designer Vests—Bulletproof

Wear Body Armor. Personal body armor will improve any officer's chances of survival in any shoot-out. Officers dying of bullet wounds to the chest should be a thing of the past. Bullet-resistant rather than

---

*The Police Weapons Center, *Ambush Attacks: A Risk Reduction Manual for Police* (Gaithersburg, Maryland, International Association of Chiefs of Police, 1974), pp. 1–29.

†Joseph Wambaugh, The Onion Field (New York, Dell Publishing, 1983), pp. 150–183.

bullet-proof, current standards have upgraded these vests to where they do stop most handgun bullets. As part of the designer concept, officers can get these garments in various bullet-stopping grades—and weights—to suit an individual's tolerance for long time periods. When a vest begins to annoy its wearer, it usually ends up in the trunk of the patrol car or the police locker room.

Chapter 9

POLICE PURSUITS AND ROADBLOCKS

Police pursuits and roadblocks are closely related. Both have the goal of apprehending a motorist who came to police attention by sudden flight when police ordered him or her to stop, by driving a car just used in the commission of a serious crime, or driving one listed as wanted. Both may end in shoot-outs and collisions—the chase at any time while in progress and the block when the fleeing motorist attempts to crash it.

It is easier to trap and stop a fleeing car, than it is to chase and stop it. Recognition of this fact is the prime mover in police efforts to develop new products that will assure rapid deployment and barriers that can be set up in minutes. The new "spike stick" is one of these products that will soon outdate old-fashioned pursuits with innovative changes in road block "hardware."

Spike sticks are light in weight and when stretched across a highway will stop a fleeing vehicle by puncturing its tires. They are functionable for this purpose as the same idea has long been in use to control traffic: DO NOT ENTER—SEVERE TIRE DAMAGE. In fact, this idea was used as early as the 1920s during Prohibition—America's "noble experiment" to restrict alcoholic beverages. State police in New York studded several pieces of 2X6 lumber with 5-inch nails and stretched them across the highway to deflate the tires of trucks carrying whiskey across the border from Canada for sale in New York City.

A far greater improvement would be the adaption of the "ignition interlock" device used as part of the sentencing of a DUI repeater. This device is installed on the repeat offender's car and he or she must blow in it when they start their car. If the device registers a BAC close to the legal limit, the car will not start. The ideal adaption is a device that can be installed in police cars, and—when operated—will stop a fleeing vehicle within a few hundred yards!

Engineers knowledgeable about the ignition interlock device might join with colleagues in the photo radar or laser speed monitoring fields to work out a delivery system to shut off the ignition of a fleeing vehicle.

Police Pursuits

The California Highway Patrol defines a police pursuit as an event involving one or more law enforcement officers attempting to apprehend a suspect operating a motor vehicle while the suspect is trying to avoid arrest by using high-speed driving or other evasive tactics.

In recent years, there have been strong suggestions from public officials and influential community leaders to ban police pursuits under any circumstances. These pleas for stoppage are usually linked to a recent traffic accident in which the fleeing vehicle totals a car loaded with passengers or the pursuing police car is in a collision with an "innocent bystander" car in its path.

Police pursuits are obviously dangerous, but to allow no pursuits would destroy a major goal of policing—catching criminals. "Catch them later" is the plea of stoppage adherents. It is not always possible to do so promptly, and what about crimes committed in this period? "Modify pursuit policy" is often a secondary plea, adding "No high-speed pursuits for minor traffic violations."* However, the pursuing officer has no way of knowing why this driver is trying to avoid arrest. He or she may run because the car's four occupants have been robbing banks on the average of one a week for several weeks and have guns and ski masks in the car—not to avoid a stop sign citation.

In general, most jurisdictions are making their pursuits as safe as possible by establishing a clear and concise policy for the conduct of pursuits, introducing a supervisor into the chase team while the chase is in progress, and by frequent hands-on training sessions to enhance the high-speed driving skills of all officers on patrol and traffic duty.

Policy for Pursuits. A written policy for conducting pursuits should have as its theme: Do not initiate a pursuit if the dangers of pursuing or continuing a pursuit are too great (weather/road conditions, heavy vehicle and/or pedestrian traffic, or when violator's vehicle can easily outperform the police car or motorcycle). Major segments should include when a pursuit can be initiated, when it can be aborted, and the roles of the primary and secondary pursuit units.

A more controversial segment, in California, reads: "Unless a greater hazard would result, a pursuit should not be undertaken if the sub-

---

*"Let's Get Serious About Police Pursuits!" *Traffic Safety,* Vol. 93 No. 3 (May/June 1993) pp 26–27.

ject(s) can be identified to the point where later apprehension can be accomplished."

Command of Pursuits. Field supervisors of the rank of sergeant or higher shall be assigned to pursuits. Upon being notified of the pursuit and his or her assignment, this supervisor should join or monitor the pursuit and notify the dispatcher of his or her acceptance of full supervisory responsibility. The officer who first attempts to stop the fleeing vehicle is in charge of the pursuit until the assigned supervisor can take over.

Within the supervisor's role in police pursuits are decisions as to establishing road blocks, setting out spike sticks, and authorizing forcible stops (channelization, ramming, boxing-in, or the use of firearms).

Training in High-Speed Driving. At least annually and, if possible, twice a year, a hands-on class in driving skills should be scheduled. The length of this instructional session depends on local resources to replace men and women attending the session. Curriculum development should be aimed at solving ongoing problem areas.

In New York City, the first class of this type was held in a huge parking lot at a beach on the outskirts of the city. Public access was blocked, but this was no problem as it was held on three days in the middle of winter. The instructors were a professor from New York University's Safety Center and three officers who moonlighted as stock-car drivers at nearby race tracks. Unfortunately, the first day during mock pursuits at high speeds one of the students was killed. The right front wheel of his almost-new car collapsed and the vehicle flipped over several times, and the young man died several hours later. Some days later, the head of the Traffic Division convinced the Police Commissioner to reschedule the school for the next week. All went well as planned, with good results apparent on the street—the young officer's death highlighted the fact that pursuit driving was hazardous and life-threatening! It proved to be excellent motivation to learn more about it among all the students.

Roadblocks

Roadblocks should not be confused with "vehicle checks," wherein one or more officers station themselves on a road to stop most of the passing vehicles, primarily to inspect the vehicles' safety equipment. A roadblock is a police technique generally aligned with the apprehension of felons. It is a technique of using police personnel and equipment to restrict the use of a roadway at one or more selected locations for the specific purpose of preventing the escape of criminals.*

Basically, roadblocks are a police adaption of the military concept of encirclement. Militarily, the word *cordon* was used to describe a line or series of soldiers placed at intervals, or of military forts enclosing an area to prevent passage of unauthorized persons.

The circular roadblock system is often employed with excellent results. The point where a bank robbery, kidnapping, or other serious crime occurs is used as the center of a circle. A circle is then drawn on a map of the area. The radius of the circle will be governed by the length of time between the time the crime was committed and the time road blocks can be established.

Patrol cars are placed so as to block every avenue of escape out of the circle; within the circle, other cars are placed to patrol the roads in search of the wanted car and to put service station operators and others on the lookout for it.

The circular roadblock system is utilized to completely bottle up suspects within a given area. In the application of this encirclement method, every possible avenue of escape must be considered and road-blocked. Two separate and distinct circular roadblock systems, referred to as the inner circle and the outer circle, have also been used successfully.

In the operation of the inner circle technique, the circling of the immediate scene of the crime attempts to effectively "bottle up" the subjects. The purpose of the inner circle blocks are to speedily block the area surrounding the crime and drive the subjects off main roads, where they may become lost, where they may be more readily observed in sparsely populated areas, where roads or condition of roads will not permit high-speed travel, and where roads do not permit travel in any one direction for any great distance.

In the operation of the outer circle technique, the radius of which is usually several miles larger than the inner circle, blocks are set up on principal highways and at principal intersections. The purpose of the outer circle is to apprehend the fleeing criminals if they have fled the area covered by the inner circle.†

A semiencirclement method is often employed when sufficient police

---

*Roadblock techniques may be used to restrict entry to a disaster area, but this is no more than a "screening" roadblock to prevent tourists and sightseers from entering the area and hampering rescue efforts.

†John I. Schwartz, *Police Roadblock Operations* (Springfield, Thomas, 1962), pp. 28–29.

manpower is not available for circular roadblocking systems. It is sometimes effective in impromptu situations, especially where the number of escape arteries available to the fleeing subjects are limited and police officials use good judgment in selecting the escape routes to be blocked.

The "blockade" at roadblocks consists of flares, warning ("Stop Ahead—Police"), and stop signs ("Stop—Police"), and one or more police cars parked to partially block the roadway to identify the operation as a police roadblock. Improvised materials, such as trucks or heavy cargo materials, have had a mixed reception among police officials planning roadblock operations; many of them believe these physical obstructions invite suicidal acts—some fleeing criminals have increased their speeds on view of such obstructions and deliberately crashed into them.

In selecting the blockade point, if the choice is optional, a place where the area adjacent to the roadway is restricted, such as a bridge, culvert, or cut through a hill, should be selected. However, clear visibility in either direction is mandatory. Do not select a blockade point which will not enable a motorist to see the roadblock in time to stop. A roadblock should *not* be established just over the crest of a hill, behind a sharp curve, or where an access road intercepts the highway within sight distance of the blockade point.

All radio communications about the location of roadblocks should always be in code, whether it is the place to be blocked or the report of some action by blocking officers, as fleeing criminals are sometimes in the possession of radio equipment capable of receiving local police calls.

The safety and the convenience of the motoring public, as well as the safety of the officers, is of prime importance in planning the location of the blockade. Consideration must be given to the placing of signs, flares, or other devices to permit motorists sufficient time to stop at all blocked points. The location must be carefully selected with emphasis on good visibility in both directions. At night, sufficient illumination must be provided. Flares of an acceptable type should be used to mark the approach, and the patrol car or cars used in the roadblock should be placed in a position where police insignia can be illuminated sufficiently so as to be recognizable. At night, this may be accomplished by choosing locations with overhead lighting for blockade points, or utilizing the headlights or spotlight of a patrol vehicle, or by the use of portable light plants.

Officers not normally engaged in traffic enforcement must be trained in acceptable techniques and methods used to stop vehicles by hand signals or flashlight. Signals transmitted by flashlight must be given more slowly to be seen and understood by motorists at night. Confusing signals by untrained officers at any time could have disastrous results.

Police units containing less than two officers should not be assigned to roadblocks. If it becomes necessary to assign units containing only one officer, several units should be provided for a single location.

There is no safe way to block a road or highway. Someone must be exposed to danger if the blockade is to function thoroughly and efficiently. However, as few officers as possible should expose themselves. Since one officer will have to make an inspection of cars and their occupants, the other officers should take advantage of any cover, keeping their fellow officer and the vehicles stopped under constant observation. All officers, and particularly the inspecting officer, should use the flashlight, whistle, etc., in their "weak" hands to leave their "gun" hands free at all times.

When it is necessary to blockade a two-lane road and stop traffic traveling in only one direction, the units should be parked at a forty-five-degree angle to the roadway, partially blocking the lane used by the traffic to be stopped (see Figs. 9A–D). Appropriate warning signs or devices should be placed in the approximate center of the roadway, not less than 300 feet from the unit facing the traffic to be stopped. Warning signs should be in letters of sufficient size and luminosity to be readable at a distance of not less than 150 feet either in daylight or darkness.

At the "stop point" of the blockade, a sign should be placed on the approximate center line of the roadway displaying the word "STOP" in letters of sufficient size and luminosity to be readable at a distance of not less than 150 feet either in daylight or darkness. (A standard *stop* sign would be appropriate for this purpose.) At the same point of the blockade, at least one lighted red light should be placed at the side of the roadway clearly visible to the oncoming traffic at a distance of not less than 300 feet.

While the "stop point" officer is checking the stopped vehicle, the second officer should take cover with a firearm on the opposite side of the patrol car, using the engine of the unit as a shield, and keeping the entire scene covered.

In stopping traffic going in both directions, the same system may be used only if the traffic is light. In heavy traffic areas, it is necessary to assign two units to stop traffic going in both directions, with the second unit parking the same as the first, except on the opposite side of the road approximately 250 feet away (see Fig. 9-B).

Any roadblock on a main traveled highway causes great congestion

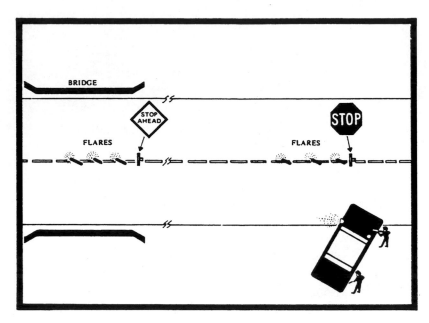

Figure 9-A. Roadblock: one lane, two-lane roadway.

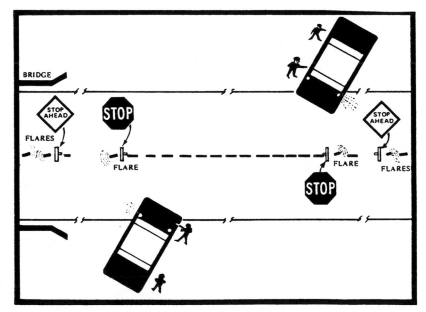

Figure 9-B. Roadblock: both directions, two-lane highway.

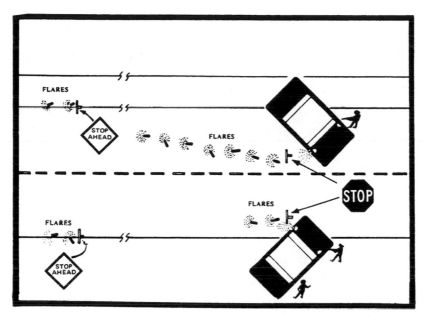

Figure 9-C. Roadblock: one direction, multilane roadway.

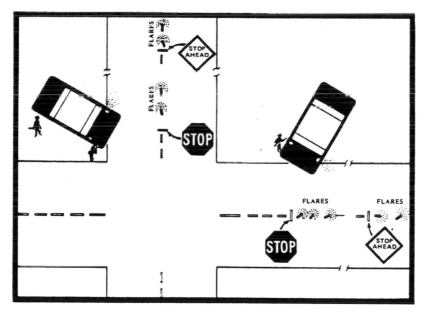

Figure 9-D. Roadblock: two directions, intersection.

and should be avoided if possible. When establishing a roadblock on a freeway or expressway, select a location where traffic can be diverted off the main roadway onto an off-ramp for "stop point" inspection and then back onto the main highway via an on-ramp. This necessitates traffic control where the off-ramp and on-ramp intersect with the street or road carrying traffic at right angles to the highway from which the traffic was diverted. Otherwise, the roadblock of one side of a multilane highway is the same as a blockade of one lane of a two-lane roadway; however, the warning sign should be placed a minimum of 500 feet from the blockade point facing the traffic to be stopped. At least two such signs should be used and placed on either side of the roadway. In addition, flares or other regulatory devices should be placed in a position to funnel traffic into one lane (see Fig. 9-C).

Blocking a four-lane intersection properly requires at least two units and four officers. It is almost impossible for two officers to block such an intersection with any degree of safety or efficiency. If two units are used, blocking traffic in two directions, the same system as outlined above may be employed, placing a unit on each road to be blocked (see Fig. 9-D).

"Covering" officers, in position behind the patrol vehicle, should not be hidden from approaching cars, as they are strong motivation for all approaching motorists to obey the roadblock's "stop" signs and the stop signals of the "Stop Point" officer. This officer should be positioned in full view, but with a planned exit route to safety in the event of "aimed cars"—vehicles driven to run down the officer. This officer should stop cars before they come alongside, examine them visually before bringing them forward for a final check, and keep a sufficient distance from the car to avoid physical seizure by its occupants. If hostilities develop, this officer should "hit the dirt" to get out of the line of fire of his covering officers.

Each car stopped should be inspected and the occupants investigated. The officer as "Stop Point" must look in the car. The fugitive may be hiding on the floor with a gun on the driver. If any occupant of the car arouses suspicion, identification should be verified in some manner. When suspicion warrants a detailed check of the occupants of a car, the "Stop Point" officers should order the driver to park at the "Stop Point," or at a place previously selected for such examination.

An officer should be under observation of no less than one other officer in a position of support before proceeding with this examination. When covered, the officer should approach the operator from the left and rear of the vehicle and order the occupants from the car with their hands exposed; the officer should have his/her service revolver or other firearm at the ready position. When there are two or more suspects, they should be ordered to stand together with their hands raised and face away from the officer. A fair warning should be given against any false motions or threatening gestures. The officer should then proceed to conduct a search, beginning with the closest suspect. When the search of the first suspect is completed, direct the person to walk just beyond the others, then search the next individual, continuing this procedure until all have been searched. By conducting a search in this manner, the officer remains at all times in the rear of the suspects and is in a position to fully observe any menacing movement. After a thorough search of each suspect, they should be directed to stand in an area exposed to the observations of the covering officer. While this officer maintains watch, a search of the suspect's vehicle can be conducted. When dealing with potentially armed criminals, the officer must be extremely cautious and must not at any time be placed between the suspects and the covering officer.

All officers participating in a roadblock should be on the same side of the block to insure that there will be no crossfire. They should decide beforehand to which side of the block all officers will go in the event it becomes necessary to take cover. It is very dangerous to have officers on both sides of a roadblock unless separated by a sufficient distance and so positioned as to their field of fire that there would be no possibility of crossfire in the event of any shoot-out. Generally, a one-sided or triangular field of fire offers safety against the hazard of crossfire. All officers firing in one direction is a technique of great safety; officers firing from the corners of a triangle's base line toward a central apex at least thirty to forty feet distant also affords effective safety against damaging crossfire.

Ample firepower is a must at roadblocks. The 12-gauge shotgun with the #00 buckshot load is the most versatile weapon available to the officer for use at roadblocks. It has a distinct psychological advantage over other types of weapons and can, in many instances, be used to good advantage without need of actual firing. Extreme caution must be exercised by covering officers in firing these weapons. Buckshot patterns, even at close range, can be broad enough to cause injury or death to a "Stand Point" officer caught between a suspect car and his covering officers.

Safety in the use of firearms cannot be overemphasized. When the use of firearms becomes *necessary,* officers should aim and fire deliberately, remembering that it is better not to fire at all than to endanger the lives of citizens or fellow officers.

It is vitally important for a police officer to know when he may lawfully use his gun. If he kills without proper justification, then he may be prosecuted for murder or manslaughter as well as be sued by the family of the deceased. "When to shoot," is particularly applicable to officers assigned to roadblocks.

When one or more of the occupants of a car stopped at a roadblock opens fire on the "Stop Point" or covering officers, or both, the officers have a legal right to defend themselves, exercising care in their firing not to wound any unarmed occupants of the stopped car. Any occupant could be an unwilling hostage.

The most difficult problem dealing with the officer's right to use deadly force arises when the officer *suspects* that a person has committed a felony and seeks to arrest the person. When the officer acts only on suspicion, as may be the case where a person acts suspiciously when stopped at a blockade, the majority of the courts has held that the officer is taking a risk and has refused to justify the use of deadly force if the suspect turns out to be an innocent person. The reason for this rule is that human life is too sacred to be placed in danger without sufficient reason.

These roadblocks are termed stop-and-search operations as they process many cars through the block until they find the one being sought. Therefore, the use of "speed sticks" to lacerate — and deflate — the tires of a single vehicle is not desirable. These devices, however, may be useful as an adjunct to the roadblock to quickly stop a motorist who suddenly steps on the gas and takes off, or makes a U turn as they first sight the block.

Chapter 10

TRAFFIC DIRECTION

The best police tool to secure some degree of control in congested downtown areas or along heavily traveled roadways is police traffic direction. This basic function may be necessary to meet the demands of recurring congestion (known choke areas/bottlenecks), and nonrecurring congestion (accidents/disabled vehicles). Known choke areas and bottlenecks require the skills of traffic engineers in modifying the existing roadway configurations causing the congestion. During the 2- or 3-year delay common in these roadway changes, the police must direct and redirect traffic in these areas. Police have long performed very well in reducing congestion in and around accidents or the blocking of highway lanes by disabled vehicles by rapid response time, efficient servicing of an accident or disabled-vehicle blockage, and prompt clearance of the scene and the resumption of regular traffic flow.*

Police direction of traffic has a long history, until it was replaced at intersections by mechanical and electrical signals. Today, police in uniform post themselves where they can be seen and direct traffic whenever traffic signals are "out" or cannot cope with the problem of a blocked freeway or "gridlock" on city streets.

Traffic direction by police officers safely enhances the capacity of an intersection or other segment of a street and highway system by the following:

1. Signalling traffic with arm-and-hand and possibly audio signals to stop and start, or if the intersection is controlled with a traffic signal, by maintaining obedience to the signal or taking over control when the mechanical signal is unable to handle the volume of traffic emergencies.
2. Adjudicating left-turn movement of vehicles in the face of opposing traffic by utilizing gaps in the approaching stream of traffic

---

*R. P. Russell, "Choke Areas", *Police Chief,* Vol. 56. No. 7 (July 1989), p. 21–25.

when an oncoming car does not present an immediate hazard to the turning vehicle.

3. Assisting right-turn movement of vehicles to merge with safety into the stream of pedestrians and cross traffic, again seeking gaps to facilitate such movement.
4. Preventing jaywalking and illegal parking within a short distance of the officer's assigned duty site.
5. Being alert to developing congestion along exits from the intersection and preventing vehicles from blocking the crossing.
6. Protecting the scene of accidents and the restricted areas of emergencies and disasters, and maintaining traffic ways for the arrival and departure of authorized emergency vehicles.

Positions for Directing Traffic

Officers assigned to intersection control or *point duty* will usually find their work to coordinate traffic movement has three major parts:

1. Officers must be able to expedite traffic flow by directing traffic units in when and how to move whenever congestion or other hazard makes traffic movement dangerous or difficult. The assigned officer assumes responsibility for manually directing traffic.
2. Emergency direction of traffic should be ready to meet unusual or unexpected conditions. Directing traffic in emergencies requires special techniques. There is a great amount of confusion at the scene of fires and other emergencies. Authorized emergency vehicles must not only be given the right-of-way, but may also require skilled traffic direction to anticipate their needs and keep lanes open at these scenes.
3. Directing officers will be asked questions on almost every possible subject. The officer is vulnerable; he is in uniform and apparently on duty. The questions must be answered courteously and rapidly, but the movement of traffic should not be blocked for this purpose.

Years ago in New York City, before the time of one-way streets, traffic policemen took a position in the center of the intersection, and traffic would alternately pass by in opposing directions in accordance with the officer's signals. Today one-way streets have complicated the problem of the best position for the police officer directing traffic, and the trend toward narrowing the lanes on a street in order to accommodate another lane of traffic has practically forced the police officer directing traffic to a position at the side or corner of an intersection.

The most common intersection in street and highway systems is the location at which two streets cross each other. Suggested traffic direction positions at these crossings are as follows:

1. ***Both Streets Two-way:*** In the center of the intersection, between the opposing streams of traffic (see Fig. 10).

2. ***One Street Two-way:*** In the center of traffic on the two-way street just inboard of the crosswalk (see Fig. 11). Many officers place themselves between lanes on a one-way street, but this is a position of danger: Lanes of traffic moving in the same direction have little clearance and some drivers change lanes without thinking.

3. ***Both Streets One-way:*** At the corner between the approaching flow of traffic on each street, moving along the inboard side of the near cross-walk as the flow of traffic changes, as may be required for the control of pedestrians and turning vehicular traffic (see Fig. 12).

These general rules of positioning in directing traffic are important at uncontrolled intersections; the major task of the police is not to guide pedestrians or turning vehicles or to start traffic after it has been stopped, but to *stop* traffic. Approaching vehicles must be able to see the officer easily or they cannot be expected to stop at his direction.

Vehicles are to be stopped by the officer's signal before they enter the intersection, at their near crosswalk's outboard line. Operating from the center of two two-way streets, an officer can accomplish this stopping procedure; motorists expect officers on traffic direction work to take this position. From this position, the officer is at most only half an intersection away from where he directs an approaching vehicle to stop. When the officer positions himself in the middle of a two-way street, but to the side of traffic on a one-way street, he is only half an intersection away from where he directs the approaching vehicle to stop at this type of crossing. When both streets are one-way at an intersection, the officer's position on the corner between the approaching traffic streams is only the width of the crosswalks from approaching traffic and in a good position to stop approaching cars.

Intersections of irregular shape and with more than the normal number of intersecting streets are a problem in positioning. It is necessary for the officer to survey the intersection, the direction of traffic flow, the number of one-way streets, and whether certain turning movements are

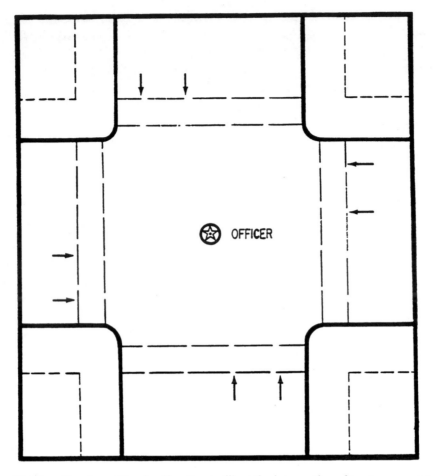

Figure 10. The officer's position for directing traffic at the intersection of two two-way streets is in the center of the intersection.

forbidden because of the shape of the intersection or other reasons. Often the intersection will contain only one major traffic stream at any one time and the officer can position himself accordingly. It may be a problem intersection at which the officer is not expected to do much more than protect himself and prevent massive traffic jams, or which requires a team of officers and special team tactics with one officer as team leader (calling the signals).

Until recently, the intersection of Park Row and Center Street in New York City was one of these classic problem intersections. It was a heavily traveled two-way street with two lanes of traffic in each direction bisected by a four-lane one-way street and joined to the four-lane divided high-

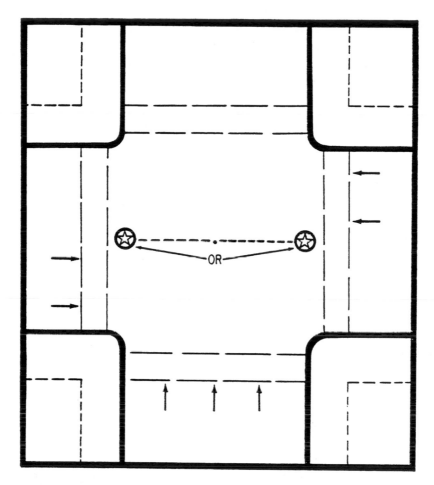

Figure 11. The officer should take an unbalanced or off-center position when only one of the streets at an intersection is one-way. He should be on either edge of the one-way traffic stream.

way traffic of the Brooklyn Bridge! Officers did the best they could, sometimes manning all three suitable and safe positions, and tried to keep the intersection open—the mayor used this intersection about ten times a day to reach his office in New York's City Hall.

Once positioned, an officer should move only within reasonable limits. The "never-step-back" rule originated in the days when all streets were two-way and the officer's position was always in the center of the intersection. To step back meant the officer might be struck by a vehicle; it is still an excellent rule for all officers directing traffic today. It may not be important when working close to a corner or along the inboard side of a crosswalk, but developing the habit of not making any radical

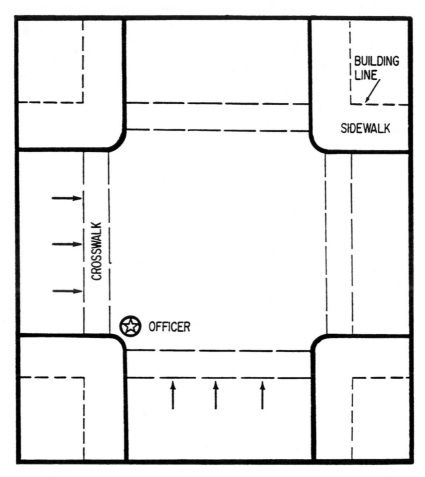

Figure 12. A safe position for an officer directing traffic at the intersection of two one-way streets is on the edge of the one-way traffic stream at the corner.

backward movement is a necessity for the days an officer is working between lanes of moving traffic when a backward step could move him into a position of hazard. It has been alleged that the unpopularity of small platforms to raise the officer above traffic for improved visibility developed from officers' forgetting their raised position and falling into the path of an oncoming car when they stepped back.

One of the major functions of traffic direction at intersections in a downtown area is to prevent an intersection from being blocked by vehicles moving into the intersection when traffic is heavy and being trapped when cars ahead come to a stop. While many cities enforce local vehicle code regulations against blocking intersections, the traffic conditions of downtown areas confuse motorists. The service of a citation for this violation at a time of heavy traffic movement does not contribute to a solution of the immediate problem of congestion. Officers must be alert for midblock obstructions, such as double-parking or a disabled vehicle, and should continually observe the *exits* of the intersection for developing signs of congestion. In watching for the factors which will reduce traffic movement through an intersection, an officer is not forced into making any sudden stop signals in order to prevent the oncoming vehicle from blocking the intersection, which might cause a rear-end collision two or three cars behind the stopped vehicle.

New York City's original group of police officers assigned to direct traffic at intersections were known as "the Broadway Squad." Every officer was at least six feet, two inches tall. Assignments were at major intersections along the midtown segment of Broadway. The squad earned a reputation for stopping runaway horses. While the traffic problem is now different from that in the days of horsedrawn vehicles, many police administrators believe officers who are above average height have an advantage in directing traffic.

Visibility is a vital factor for the safety of police officers directing traffic. Poor light conditions, blue police uniforms, black raincoats, and inclement weather have contributed to many injuries and deaths among policemen on traffic duty. Police safety equipment for officers assigned to such duty is usually purchased by the police unit and includes crossbelts and gloves of reflecting material that will pick up the lights of approaching vehicles and clearly indicate the officer standing in the highway.

Lighting at an intersection is an important factor in police safety; a better than average amount of white light can be provided for intersections manned by police simply by increasing the illumination installed in existing light standards. Officers who find poor illumination at intersections at which they are assigned during the hours of dusk and darkness should report this fact and seek the help of their supervisor in securing an increase in the existing illumination or the installation of a special bank of spotlights.

In emergencies, the warning light system of police vehicles and flares serve to warn approaching cars under any conditions of visibility, and an officer can use his flashlight for better identification by motorists and to supplement his signals. Rain lowers the visibility potentiality of any driver. The drivers requiring glasses have a dual problem during rainstorms: fogged-up windshields and clouded glasses. Officers should not be caused to endanger their lives by attempting to direct traffic under poor conditions of visibility.

Basic Signals: Stopping and Starting Traffic

Signals used by police for the direction of traffic should have some uniformity. Some officers direct traffic in a robust manner, suggesting an unusual interest in body-building. On the other hand, one New York City officer appeared to be using wrist and finger signals rather than arm and hand gestures. Officers should seek to be uniform in their gestures for directing traffic. The unusual disturbs motorists and might contribute to an accident.

The basic signal to stop is an upraised hand at the end of an extended arm raised to well above shoulder level, with the palm of the hand clearly facing the approaching driver for whom the signal is intended (see Fig. 13). Some police departments ask officers making this signal to point at the approaching car with the extended arm prior to raising the palm into the stop signal. This is fine signalling when there is only one lane of approaching traffic, but difficult when there are many lanes of traffic. Also, the officer's pointing hand often merges into his silhouette to the driver approaching the intersection. The raised-palm signal is above shoulder level, and for this reason and the breadth of the hand it is a more visible signal. (When the traffic officer has on white gloves it is a distinctive signal and quite visible.)

An officer directing traffic on crossings with one or more two-way streets, and seeking to move it along through the intersection, will frequently signal stop with both hands after having partially stopped traffic in one direction with the right hand. They do this by holding both hands out and up from the shoulders in the stop position until all approaching traffic has halted.[1] Instructors in many police academies object to this two-handed stop signal, saying it is better to stop traffic in one direction effectively before attempting to stop opposing traffic.

When bulky vehicles such as station wagons and trucks are the first vehicles to stop in the lane nearest the police officer's position in the intersection, it may be necessary for him to move slightly in front of the stopped vehicle, which because of its bulk is blocking the view of drivers in other lanes and preventing them from seeing the officer, in order to display the stop signal to all approaching drivers.

The signal for a stopped vehicle to start moving begins at shoulder

Figure 13. The *stop* signal for directing traffic: The hand is above shoulder level and is pointed at approaching cars.

level, with the officer extending the arm toward the stopped vehicle (pointing) and waving the car onward by bending the arm at the elbow and drawing the hand toward the chest (see Fig. 14). Once traffic in one direction starts to move, the officer turns and faces opposing traffic and delivers the same signal. The officer need not wait until all cars have complied with this signal. He can turn and deliver the same signal to the opposing traffic with some promptness. Therefore there is no justification for signalling cars to start with both hands at the same time, nor is there justification for rapidly repeating this start signal, as many motorists will interpret it as a speed-up signal.

The signal to pull up to a position indicated by the officer on duty directing traffic at an intersection is usually reserved for turning traffic

Figure 14. The *start* signal is a "come along" motion made in the direction of traffic movement.

facing opposing vehicular or pedestrian traffic. It is started by the officer pointing with either hand to the position at which the driver should pull his stopped or slowly approaching vehicle. It is completed by motioning the driver forward, usually by dropping the pointing arm toward the selected position as the vehicle moves closer to the officer. If possible, the pointing hand and arm are kept in position, serving to hold the turning vehicle until conditions are safe for the turning movement.

Signal for Turning Traffic

Left-turning traffic at intersections manned by a police officer directing traffic depends upon the police officer to adjudicate the immediate hazard factor. He should indicate to them that it is safe for turning by a come along motion, or that it is unsafe by either a slightly extended stiff arm movement (usually started at waist level) indicating "position here," or by raising the palm of the hand (still at waist level) slightly toward the approaching car and indicating "stop here." A standard full stop signal at above shoulder level should not be made, as it might confuse the approaching driver and other motorists in nearby lanes.

When the officer decides it is safe for the motorist to complete the turn, he stops opposing traffic with the regular stop signal and motions the left-turning motorist to complete turning by making a modified come along signal with the other hand. When standing in the center of an intersection, the officer will position left-turning vehicles and direct their movement in front of him/her (before they reach the officer's position in the center of the intersection). When necessary on two-way streets, the officer can have two lanes of left-turning traffic turning safely.

Right-turning traffic requires little or no traffic direction unless such traffic is crossing a heavily traveled crosswalk or has to merge into heavy vehicular traffic. In such cases, the officer utilizes similar signals to hold the turning car until it is safe to turn, then directs it into the turning motion as he/she stops and holds approaching traffic with the other hand and arm. Natural gaps, when available, are utilized to clear turning vehicles; some officers have developed skills in directing turning vehicles before they deliver a signal to start traffic moving straight ahead or after they have stopped through traffic.

Whistle Signals

Officers directing traffic should not shout at motorists, but may whistle at them. It sounds odd, but for many years New York's finest officers used a very distinctive traffic whistle to announce their arm and hand signals. It was a necessity when most of New York's intersections were not signalized.

These whistle signals were as follows:

1. A single long blast means *stop*.
2. Two short blasts mean *start*.

3. Three or more short blasts, with very short intervals, mean *emergency stop.*

The short blasts, rapidly given with only a very short interval, were very useful to stop all traffic on the approach of an authorized emergency vehicle, to stop a car that had committed a violation but had driven past the officer and the intersection, and to warn a motorist bent on illegal parking.

Flashlight Signals

During periods of dusk and darkness an officer will find a flashlight useful in directing traffic. This light is particularly appropriate at accident scenes, as motorists do not expect to encounter officers in the highway directing traffic. Officers shine the light on the pavement in front of approaching cars as a stop signal and move the light in a small "come along" arc to indicate that the vehicle is to start or continue to move.

Route Policing: Peak Traffic

The necessity of getting to and from work each working day puts a great number of commuters on the highway. Resorting more and more to auto use, these workers may drive alone or ride as a part of a car pool. They are responsible for the congestion of the highways and local roads during the morning and afternoon peak periods.

In connection with route policing, the police executive must make a policy decision as to the precedence of handling traffic by origin. Some communities are adverse to making it any easier for outsiders to get into the city. They believe that their parkways and expressways are for the use of local taxpayers riding to and from work. For this reason any cutting off of in-town access roads on parkways and expressways to divert local traffic to other major arterial roads is resented by local residents.

Police executives must point toward a route policing theory during peak hours of traffic flow. Personnel must be concentrated on traffic direction to assist traffic into the city in the morning and aid it in its homeward journey at night.

Available police should be assigned to key intersections and merging points noted for heavy volumes of traffic along the major routes into the city during the morning peak period. They should be assigned to similar posts during the afternoon peak, but along routes leading outward from the downtown area. The officer's task in this route policing is to facilitate the flow of traffic by adequate traffic direction.

Cars disabled as the result of mechanical failure are ruinous to the capacity of a highway at any time, but when they occur during periods of heavy volume their potential for blocking traffic and causing accidents is sufficiently high to warrant police action to detect their presence and direct their prompt removal. The problem of disabled cars includes cars stalled due to a flat tire or mechanical failure and cars on the roadway due to a conflict in an accident. Locked bumpers are particularly common in any high-density traffic stream.

At accident scenes an officer should have a formalized procedure of setting out flares and parking the police vehicle in order to achieve maximum notice to approaching vehicles and top protection to persons and vehicles involved in the accident. Officers should expect passing motorists to want to help. If the officer can utilize them it will be necessary to direct their efforts.

Many police units instruct their officers directing traffic at accident scenes to get the parked cars of the curious out of the way, along with their occupants. Officers should also expect passing motorists who do not stop to slow down and become less aware of their driving and the safe operation of their vehicles while they attempt to view the accident scene in detail. Appropriate "come along" signals will get them moving.

In servicing an accident scene late at night or early in the morning, particularly between midnight and five in the morning on Saturday and Sunday, the officer's position directing traffic should be as far out of the approaching stream of traffic as possible. The officer should also be alert for the drunken driver. (Officers must move when the first beelike buzz of the approaching vehicle is detected.)

The major objectives of such traffic duty are to prevent secondary accidents, to open up the traffic stream for the approach of authorized emergency vehicles and facilitate their departure from the scene, and to keep the scene free for evidence searches, the interviewing of participants and other witnesses, and the activity of tow trucks. Subliminally, there is a duty to prevent theft from the cars or the persons involved in the accident.

Freeway Incident Management (FIM)

An effective freeway incident management (FIM) plan is now common in most agencies with interstate highway mileage. The simple goal of a FIM plan is to lessen the time that one or two lanes of a freeway are blocked because of an accident or other mishap.

The major components of such a plan are: detection and verification of blockage event, response time, on-site management of event, clearance time, and motorist information. The key component is information. Providing accurate and timely information to the public at the beginning of the event will cause many motorists to self-divert and reduce the traffic problem at the scene.

The frequency of these accidents suggests timely evaluation aimed at improvement in the timespan without diminishing essential high-quality service.*

Traffic Direction at Disasters

While accident scenes have an attendant problem of the curiosity of the passing motorists, the scene of other emergencies attracts people who will drive miles to get to the scene of the emergency to satisfy their curiosity or become looters. Some of these individuals will leave their cars anywhere in their urge to get closer to the scene, and officers on traffic duty at emergency scenes must be alert to this attempt to park vehicles in locations which will add to the traffic congestion common at these emergencies. Unbelievably, these strongly motivated curious persons will park their cars and sneak through yards and alleys and over low-roofed buildings to reach the actual scene of the emergency, and thus create problems for police performing first aid and rescue work, protecting property from theft, and gathering evidence.

At these scenes, traffic officers are usually well outside the core area of the emergency. Their major job objective is to clear a path for authorized emergency vehicles, to keep unauthorized vehicles out of the restricted area of the emergency, to expedite the flow of traffic generally, and to combat the problem of thrill and curiosity seekers.

At traffic posts in connection with extensive disasters officers will have a problem in screening persons who claim to be personally involved in

---

*R. P. Miner, "Freeway Incident Management", *Police Chief*, Vol. 59, No. 7 (July 1992), pp. 15, 109–20, 22–23.

the emergency. The officer directing traffic may have to service a priority pass system for entrance into an outer restricted area and check passes or travel authorizations prior to permitting entry to the inner area. In some cases, when widespread looting is reported at the disaster scene, the traffic control officer may have a secondary antitheft duty in relation to vehicles exiting from the vicinity of the disaster while the looting is in progress and for short periods after its termination.

Freeway Fog Management

Multivehicle accidents due to reduced visibility because of fog have forced freeway police into a new dimension of traffic direction: closing down the foggy area of the freeway. This is a difficult decision on a highway built to move people and cargo.

In Great Britain, police have long used various metering devices to measure the density of the fog (as photo meters measure the light), located these devices in stations on their main roads (motorways), and made attendant police responsible for taking action—usually posting warnings. The British Home Office has developed (under contract) two devices to monitor visibility in fogs: A point visibility meter (PVM) which measures the density of fog, and a background light meter (BLM). These two instruments are used together so that the calculated visibility properly reflects the perception of objects in fog.*

In America, police now use newly-developed devices to determine the density of fog but still rely upon the judgment of officers on patrol in the area. Fog can be easily measured for one locality, as at an airport, but along a stretch of highway it is very difficult because of its "patchy" nature: pockets of heavy fog.

The first control measure is warnings, but motorists usually ignore them (as long as they can see the taillights of the car ahead). The second strategy is to run "caravans" of vehicles headed by police cars at slow speed through the fog. This has proven a successful technique but places a heavy responsibility on the police officer driving the lead car. Last, the only safe control may be closure of the fog-bound segments of the freeway. There is a great deal of planning involved in this closure: (1) how best to move vehicles off the freeway and to a safe haven (near-by community with "services"—gasoline, food, lodging) and (2) how best to

---

*R. F. Syms, "Fog Detection On Motorways," *Police Research Bulletin,* No. 32 (Spring 1979), pp. 19–29.

detour vehicles intent on entering these freeway segments. Such planning should include no less than: notice and timely information to motorists by freeway radio station, prepositioned lighted directional signs (amber or other color with high visibility in fog), and an adequate* amount of equipment and personnel.

Special budget funds should be available to police for these operations from the freeway administration, and personnel and equipment should be made available to work with police. There is little doubt that these fog-related operations are cost-effective in comparison with the costs in human life and suffering of a 40- or 50-vehicle accident—and the litigated costs for failure to prevent it.

---

*More than planners usually specify.

Chapter 11

PEDESTRIAN AND BICYCLING SAFETY

Pedestrians and bicyclists are the "lightweights" of police traffic control and highway safety. They are hopelessly outweighed by the bus, truck, passenger car, and motorcycle. When pedestrians and bicyclists are in a collision with a motor vehicle, the speed of the vehicle upon impact with the lighter and smaller pedestrian or bicyclist must be added to the weight of the motor vehicle in evaluating impact energy upon the pedestrian or bicyclist. Usually it is more than sufficient to seriously injure or kill both the pedestrian and the bicyclist (as well as demolish the bicycle involved).

To point up the disparity between these lightweight traffic units and motor vehicles is the fact that even when a bicyclist strikes a stopped or slow moving motor vehicle, the impact can result in serious injury and death to the bicyclist.

Types of Pedestrian and Bicyclist Accidents

The U.S. Department of Transportation's National Highway Traffic Safety Administration (NHTSA) have evaluated reports from many states concerned with the identification of specific types of pedestrian and bicyclist accidents. NHTSA now identifies the following common types of pedestrian and bicycle accidents in urban areas of the United States:

1. *Dartout:* The pedestrian or bicyclist is exposed only a short time to the driver not at an intersection.
2. *Intersection Dash:* The pedestrian or bicyclist tries to make a quick crossing at or near an intersection.
3. *Attention Conflict:* The driver of a turning vehicle concentrates attention on traffic in one direction and strikes a pedestrian or bicyclist approaching from the other direction.
4. *Multiple Threat:* The driver's view of the pedestrian or bicyclist is blocked by other cars stopped to give the pedestrian or bicyclist the right of way.

119

5. **Bus Stop Related:** The pedestrian is struck by a vehicle after stepping out from in front of a stopped bus.
6. **Vendor—Ice Cream Truck:** The pedestrian is struck going to or from a street vendor of ice cream.
7. **Backing Up:** The driver fails to detect the pedestrian or bicyclist when backing up.*

Pedestrian Safety

Pedestrians rank after the occupants of motor vehicles as the largest category of fatalities in traffic accidents. The thousands of pedestrian deaths now approximate 20 percent of the total annual highway death toll.

One of the basic thrusts of a pedestrian safety program is to assure the safe movement of pedestrians on streets and highways shared with motor vehicles, particularly at intersections in urban areas having many points of conflict between pedestrians and motor vehicles. This reduction of conflict calls for the physical separation of pedestrians and vehicles by such means as overpasses, underpasses, skyways, pedestrian malls, and other physical countermeasures in roadway design and the use of traffic control devices likely to contribute to this physical separation of pedestrians and vehicles.

Police traffic officers and the executives of police agencies can initiate action leading to the separation of pedestrians and vehicles or the reduction of conflict between these two traffic units.

Any action initiated by police should be based on an analysis of the pattern of pedestrian-vehicle accidents at a given location. Once the pattern of accidents has been identified, the action taken must be responsive to accident causation. One or more of the following actions may serve to reduce pedestrian-vehicle accidents:

1. Paint crosswalk lines, and (if warranted) install pedestrian barriers.
2. Install traffic signals or, if they are in place, add pedestrian signals. Consider a timing change or pushbutton signal actuation.
3. Construct pedestrian refuge islands, particularly if it is a wide street.
4. Provide better lighting if large numbers of accidents occur after dark.

Traffic Safety '74 (Washington, D.C., U.S. Department of Transportation, 1975), pp. 15–16.

5. Prohibit curb parking a reasonable distance back from the corner to improve visibility of both pedestrians and motorists.
6. Establish one-way traffic, or reroute through traffic to nearby major arterial streets with little pedestrian volume.
7. Establish "scramble" systems at intersections (a system where traffic control devices stop motorists in all directions, and then pedestrians can cross without conflict).

Pedestrians often ignore vehicle code provisions enacted for their safety. The term "jaywalk" is commonly used in urban areas to describe the crossing of a street carelessly and dangerously so as to be endangered by motor vehicle traffic.

Some pedestrians seem proud of their jaywalking skills and are more than willing to match their own agility against traffic hazards both at crossings and in midblock. Many drivers treat jaywalking attempts as a challenge, a gauntlet thrown down to test their driving skill, and make every attempt to prevent the jaywalker from successfully completing his crossing.

Jaywalking is particularly common in downtown areas. The majority of pedestrian safety enforcement action is taken in these areas. Officers assigned to traffic control duty at intersections are in a particularly fine position to enforce such regulations.

Pedestrians have a definite right-of-way. Intersection control officers should enforce the law concerning failure to yield the right-of-way to a pedestrian proceeding in a lawful manner, or of pedestrians failing to yield as required. The attitude of the police officer should be one of sympathetic interest in these vehicle versus pedestrian conflicts, and it is important that all officers use the utmost courtesy and tact in requesting cooperation, giving advice, or in citing offenders.

The pedestrian traffic regulations are primarily for the protection of the pedestrian, for the purpose of correcting dangerous walking habits and reducing the number of accidents involving pedestrians. A reasonable attitude on the part of officers avoids creating situations calling for arrests for disorderly conduct. Selection of flagrant offenses for the service of a citation insures against too many "not guilty" pleas.

Pedestrian accidents do not lead themselves to selective enforcement by location. They develop primarily from people's walking habits. Enforcement of pedestrian regulations in a downtown area by police who are readily available because of traffic direction assignments or on general patrol in the area due to the high-risk occupancies serves as an excellent opportunity to not only educate the offender against whom police action is directed, but also to inform and educate passing pedestrians who witness the violator-officer contact. It is on-view and active traffic law enforcement; its educational impact should be carried by observers of such action to other roadways and intersections throughout the area where accidents do occur.

Despite the increasing number of pedestrian control signals at downtown intersections with heavy volumes of pedestrian traffic, the presence of an officer directing traffic can increase traffic flow by at least 50 percent. Downtown streets in either New York or San Francisco are excellent examples of this fact. This problem of turning into a line of pedestrians is a problem in traffic control. Without channelization it is difficult to locate detectors for these turns, and even the most modern signalling systems do not attempt to detect and evaluate pedestrian traffic volume. Therefore an arbitrary time is set for turning movements, and this frequently requires modification. The only available means of modification is the traffic officer. The elimination of turning movements can solve this problem, but most of these problem intersections are so located that such prohibition would only move the problem to another location and possibly create a difficult situation at the latter intersection.

Intoxicated Pedestrians

Intoxicated pedestrians make up about 30–50 percent of the annual total of pedestrian deaths (of men and women over 14 years of age) resulting from collisions with vehicles. Drinking and walking can be a dangerous combination. The average postmortem BAC is 0.15.

There is nothing illegal in being a drunk pedestrian. However, most cities have some local law that allows police officers to take obviously drunk pedestrians into custody long enough to sober them up. Urban area police know this is the only way to reduce nighttime pedestrian-vehicle collisions in "skid row" areas. Streets are empty of daytime commercial traffic and become speedways for nocturnal motorists quite unaware of the staggering "wino" until he or she is up on their windshield staring at them.

Antispeeding patrols at night in these areas have been effective, as sober motorists can understand. Education aimed at the victims has been ineffective, as hard-drinking men and women may not drive drunk but walking after drinking is another thing.*

Bicycling Safety

Bicycling has become enormously popular, and fatal and injurious accidents of bicycle riders are on the increase. Unlike the driver or passenger in a motor vehicle, the bicyclist is *not* protected by the "armor" of the automobile. While pedestrians and motorcyclists also have this problem, the mechanics of riding a bicycle places a bicyclist above the roadway rather than walking on it, and the force of an accident's impact usually throws the bicyclist to the roadway's surface. In addition, bicycle riders do not have the minimal protection afforded by the heavy frame and leg-guard structure of a motorcycle.

State legislators have taken action recognizing the vulnerability of bicyclists, both juveniles and adults. Provisions of vehicle codes are aimed at safe behavior by both motorists and bicyclists (see Chap. 3). Each of these traffic units have a stated responsibility for reducing conflict between vehicles and bicycles. Some state and local governments have opted for separate bicycle lanes that apportion a certain part of the roadway (at its edge, usually) to bicyclists, and there is a growing recognition of the need for bicycle paths entirely separate from roadways designed for vehicle traffic.

The statistics of rising accident rates and the steadily increasing use of bicycles, particularly by adults as a mode of transportation as well as a recreational vehicle, call for improvement in vehicle code regulations and the diversion of more funds from highway construction to the construction of bicycle lanes and paths. There is also an increasing need for drafting of child-oriented legislation and safe riding programs in schools similar to the contemporary driver education programs in high schools.

Police enforcement programs for bicycle safety should be aligned with existing vehicle code regulations, but slanted toward the foregoing needs in this field. An enforcement program aimed at accident reduction should create an increased awareness among local bicyclists, motorists,

---

*Gabriel Shapiro, "The Problem of Intoxicated Pedestrians", *Traffic Safety,* Volume 93, No. 3, (May/June, 1993), pp. 7–11.

and pedestrians that police are determined to contribute as meaningfully as possible to safe bicycling in the community.

Motorized Bicycles (Mopeds)

Motorized bicycles are generally classed with nonmotorized traffic—pedestrians and bicycles. They are basically bicycles to which small motors of one or two horsepower have been added, and changes mechanically in the structure of the bicycle are usually confined to the motor drive mechanism. To date, in California, they are exempt from registration as a vehicle. Since motorcycles require vehicle registration, this places the motorized bicycle in a class with the bicycle. In addition, the California Vehicle Code groups motorized bicycles with "pedestrians, bicycles or other nonmotorized traffic" in restricting the use of freeways to this class of road users. However, the same vehicle code forbids persons operating motorized bicycles the use of bicycle lanes or paths.

Whether a motorized bicycle is basically in the class of nonmotorized traffic or should be classed as a vehicle along with motorcycles will probably be decided in the next few years. In any event, the low cost of operation of these "bikes" will no doubt contribute to their future popularity as an alternative mode of transportation for commuting to work or school, or for travel to and from local stores. Hopefully, as these motorized bicycles become more popular, legislatures will come to acknowledge the inadequacies of existing laws and will recognize motorized bicycles as transportation vehicles, and, as a consequence, will take all characteristics of this new and unusual vehicle into account.

Countermeasures focusing upon these types of accidents should be implemented and tested. Evaluation of the effectiveness of these countermeasures should lead to appropriate modifications that will make any street and highway system a safe place for pedestrians and bicyclists.

Chapter 12

ACCIDENT INVESTIGATION

A motor vehicle traffic accident occurs when a motor vehicle in motion on a public street or highway (trafficway) causes death, injury, or property damage. Fatal and critical injury accidents are usually investigated by police officers sent to the scene by radio. Personal injury accidents are frequently investigated. Property-damage-only accidents may be investigated. A growing number of police agencies are conserving manpower by sampling less serious accidents rather than attempting to investigate all of these property-damage-only or minor personal injury accidents.

The number of accidents to be investigated has not as yet been clearly delineated. Some authorities state that 90 percent of all known accidents should be investigated; others indicate that a rate of 95 percent is the minimum effective rate. The individual police executive must resolve the problem on the basis of local police problems and manpower, but every modern police unit should have an accident investigation unit regardless of its size.

The entire traffic control program may fail because of a lack of adequate and dependable information about accidents. The size of the accident investigation unit should be sufficient to investigate a meaningful number of accidents, and the total number of investigated accidents should constitute a fair representative sample of all accidents occurring in a community.

Officers using existing formalized accident investigation procedures can secure all the available facts of an accident and take prompt police action when a violation of law is found to be among the causes of the accident. Years and years of research and practice have developed procedures which will supply the police unit with information on accidents because they are devised for probing into human behavior in accident situations. Police have learned that the anatomy of an accident is keyed to one significant event in its happening, and contributing causes of accidents can be developed from this event and other direct causes.

Since the police function is primarily the protection of life and property, accident investigation must serve two general purposes: (1) securing facts upon which to base an accident prevention program and (2) determining responsibility for accidents when possible. Ascertaining the facts of accidents so that those involved can properly exercise claims under civil law is not a police function, but rather a service emanating from the availability of such facts.

The technique of investigating accidents is to go back in reconstructing the accident as far as possible from the position of final rest of the traffic unit involved and determine the multiple causations and circumstances leading to the accident situation. What are the causes that created the effect? What were the circumstances that created the environment in which the event took place? Briefly, how and why did the accident occur?

To mount and direct a specific attack on the causes of traffic accidents, the police accident investigator attempts to fix responsibility on one or more of the following: (1) the vehicle, (2) the highway, and (3) the road user.

Police officials assign personnel to collect and compile data from the reports of police accident investigators and to prepare an analysis for an improved management of the factors which have contributed to accidents in the immediate past. It has been police accident reports and meaningful statistics developed from many such reports that has led to research upon which nationwide vehicle safety requirements are now based. These same reports, along with police recommendations for physical changes in highway conditions and the installation of signs and other traffic control devices, are used to reduce accidents at high-frequency accident locations. In combination, the faults of both vehicle and highway as reported by police serving accidents in the field have served as a basic resource in highway design and engineering.

The Anatomy of an Accident

An accident is described as an event, occurrence, or happening which is unexpected or undesigned, which has an element of chance or probability, and which has undesirable or unfortunate results. Motor vehicle codes may establish a cash value on property damage to dignify a traffic accident for police investigative purposes. This minimum damage may be fifty dollars to two hundred dollars, but it does eliminate minor bumper contacts between vehicles and some fender-bending from classification as reportable accidents.

Police reject late-reported accidents unless a participant is killed or seriously injured. It is difficult or impossible to reconstruct accidents unless the police arrive at the scene or have some contact with surviving principals of the accident within a reasonable time of its occurrence. In many areas such accidents are not investigated but are filed as a "report by participant."

An anatomy of an accident as disclosed by a police investigator depends upon the facts available to the investigator at the time of his investigation. Sometimes no witnesses are available, or the scene has been altered by the removal of one or more of the vehicles involved or by the destruction of physical evidence. It is presumed that the investigator is a competent and diligent individual who will disclose and record all available facts in the course of his investigation and dissect an accident into its major parts—the chain of events.

When all possible causes of an accident have been grouped together by an investigating officer and he believes the accident would not have occurred if any one of these causes did not exist, then the investigator may have identified the combination of factors causing the accident.

On-the-scene reconstruction of a traffic accident relates accident causation to direct causes for summary police action and to identify *direct,* *mediate,* and *early* causes for ongoing studies of high-frequency accident locations and future research and analysis.

When two or more traffic units are involved in an accident, the conduct of each traffic unit is studied separately, as each traffic unit creates its own chain of events contributing to the total accident situation. In every accident one event in the chain of events is the *key event.* * This is the event that fixes a time and place for the accident. From this time and place the assigned investigator can measure other events. The major links in the chain of events making up an accident are the following:

1. Key event.
2. Perception of hazard.
3. Possible perception.
4. Point of no escape.

The *key event* is an event on the road characterizing the manner of

---

Accident Investigation, (Sacramento, CA, California Highway Patrol, 1970), p. 3–11.

occurrence of a traffic accident involving motor vehicles. It is whichever of the following events occurs first: (1) running off the road, (2) noncollision on the road, or (3) collision on the road.

Once the investigator has established the time and place of the accident from determination of the key event, he must work back along the path of the vehicle or vehicles involved and ascertain the location at which the operator sensed the approaching hazard. The driver may not comprehend or recognize the hazard in all of its implications at this point of perception, but there is a warning. The normal routine is perception, realization or recognition, decision and action.

Possible perception is a link in the accident chain dealing with the reaction of a normal person. Prompt perception occurs when possible and actual perception are very close. Maximum delayed perception occurs when actual perception is delayed until impact shock alerts the driver.

The point of no escape is that location and that time after or beyond which an accident cannot be prevented by the driver or pedestrian (traffic unit) under investigation.

There are three more links in the chain of events of an accident which must be studied for a comprehensive investigation when they are present in an accident situation:

1. Initial behavior.
2. Maximum engagement.
3. Final rest.

Initial behavior is the movement, position, or failure to signal intent of a driver or pedestrian that creates an accident-prone situation and is characterized by either unusual, illegal, improper, or hazardous behavior by the traffic unit under investigation. It is the beginning of the path of a vehicle or a pedestrian to its position of final rest.

Point of maximum engagement and *place of final rest* of the traffic units involved serve mostly to track the paths of the vehicles and give some information on impact speed. Many investigators, however, fail to develop the path of vehicles before and after engagement as a source of the *how* factor in accidents; a lesser number use these paths to assist in estimating the energies at impact.

Driver Failure

The actions by a driver contributing to an accident are observable by witnesses and participants, or they may be reconstructed from physical evidence found at the scene. Driver failure is the term for a behavioral cause of an accident and related to the approach to the accident scene, preception of the hazard, and the decisions of the driver and his action just before impact.

Any movement, position, or failure to signal intent to make a traffic maneuver that creates a dangerous situation and is either hazardous, illegal, improper, or unusual may be initial behavior of a nature justly termed a direct contribution to the accident. Of prime importance is the hazardous nature of the act. A driver who stands on his brakes and makes a panic stop in order to slow down to a speed permitting a turn into a side road certainly commits an act inherently hazardous. Turning without caution from an improper lane, merging without regard for the car behind, and like conduct are all inherently hazardous. A car exceeding the critical speed of a curve may side-hop and run off the road; a car approaching a section of road under construction may enter an unpaved roadway at a speed too fast for the uneven road and rough surface and the driver may lose control of the vehicle; a speed too fast for conditions relating to physical characteristics of the roadway, such as intersecting streets and driveways, does not permit enough time for decision making and evasive action and is therefore hazardous.

Many investigators in New York's Accident Investigation Squad have developed the "unlucky seven" as commonly encountered contributing circumstances of driver failure. These contributing circumstances brought about by the driver of one or more of the vehicles involved in an accident are as follows:

1. Improper speed.
2. Right-of-way (failure to yield).
3. Following too closely.
4. Left of center.
5. Improper turn.
6. Improper pass.
7. Ignored traffic control.

Investigators find that some insight may be gained as to the *how* of an accident by connecting the unlucky seven category best describing the driver failure contributing to an accident with the movement of the vehicle prior to the accident. The following vehicle movements are often found to be connected with unsafe driver behavior:

1. Passing.
2. Making a left turn.
3. Making a right turn.
4. Making a U-turn.
5. Slowing or stopping.
6. Pulling into traffic.
7. Backing.
8. Changing lanes.

In seeking to determine the *why* of an accident, the investigator must probe into the behavioral causes if he/she is to discover reasons for faulty decision making.

As the time span goes back from the time of impact in an accident, the facts or influences upon a person's behavior may be nebulous and difficult to identify. However, the investigation of behavioral causes and the reasons for them must go back into the time period before an accident further than is presently being explored.

The defeatist driver wouldn't point a loaded gun at his head, because suicide may not have crept into his mind, but he will play Russian roulette with a speeding auto and subconsciously invite destruction. Some drivers operate a car in a rage in the same manner as other persons may throw dishes against a wall. Only recently a prominent citizen in a large New England city smashed his car into an abutment of a bridge, and while recovering the next day, admitted being preoccupied because of the knowledge he was about to be indicted for embezzlement! The level of an emotional storm which results in a driver's operating a car at high speed without the realization that self-destruction is being invited is not known. At one level he might realize it, but at another level the realization might not impress him as being of sufficient importance to slow down or to even care about it.

The same is true of the drinking driver. His critical judgment is impaired by the intake of alcohol, but behind this fact is one that may explain the attempt to escape reality by indulgence in alcoholic beverages. The same is true of less-aware drivers. These persons may be victims of "highway hypnosis," concentration on personal affairs, or lack of sleep. They know modern controlled-access highways dull a driver's alertness. Many of these individuals relegate driving to an automated form while their consciousness is directed toward working out solutions to personal problems, and too many drivers fall asleep while driving.

The same facts apply equally to pedestrians. What forces are at work within the mind of a jaywalking pedestrian? It is known that many pedestrian-vehicle accidents result from a pedestrian's desire to commit suicide, but how many deaths occur from the "don't-give-a-damn" attitude which occurs during an emotional storm connected with wife, job, or girl friend? How many pedestrian deaths and injuries are due to drunkenness or sleepwalking?

Seldom are poor driving skills listed as a cause of an accident, despite the fact that lack of such skill has no doubt led to poor initial behavior and faulty evasive action resulting in accidents. An attitude on the part of one participant in a multiple collision which reveals a deep conviction of his own lack of responsibility for an accident is generally not recorded, but it may be indicative of an attitude of "other-fellowship." The cult of other-fellowship has been isolated as an underlying factor in accident causation. Drivers think of themselves as excellent drivers. They believe accidents happen only to other drivers and will not concede any driver failure.

To fully investigate driver failure as a contributing circumstance of an accident, it is necessary to first break down a driver's self-confidence. Most drivers make little self-identification. "I've been driving thirty years and never had an accident." "Yes, I drive fast, but I do not have accidents."

In investigating an accident, a skilled police officer should recognize this commonly held belief as a handicap in securing an honest account of the accident from any of the drivers involved. Most individuals resist identification as the cause of the accident, but when an operator is at last convinced of his direct contribution to the accident, an excellent opportunity is offered the investigator to probe deeper into human behavior in accident causation. Operators may "open up" and answer questions.

One driver remarked at this point in the emotional impact of an accident, "I didn't care if I killed myself, I'm disgusted with life. My girl just broke up with me." Another said, "Yes, I've been drinking, plenty, too—do all the time. Drink and drive fast, that's me, and I feel good when I go fast."

There is a definite emotional impact suffered by a participant in a serious accident; the individuals concerned behave in a strange, somber way. For them the reality of normal driving, of the belief that only other fellows become involved in accidents, has quite suddenly been shattered. They do not know what to say, but may tell the bare and unvarnished truth if properly questioned. These truthful statements may point directly to the *why* of accidents.

Vehicle Defects

Accident reconstruction has not been very successful in isolating mechanical failures in a vehicle as contributing to an accident. Mechanical fault or malfunction is often hidden by the damage wrought in the accident. Some vehicles without apparent defects are unsafe at any speed. A defective tire may have caused the initial behavior setting up the collision course, but when the accident investigator examines a vehicle with extensive front-end damage and a flat tire, it is difficult to isolate the preimpact condition of the tire and develop evidence of the tire failure. A defective steering assembly can certainly contribute to an accident. After an accident and extensive damage, however, it is difficult to determine when the fault happened in the accident. The detection of vehicle defects is possible. Many accident investigation squads now have contracts with agencies competent to examine vehicles for mechanical defects or utilize a mechanical expert in the police unit.

Vehicle failure is generally grouped in an accident investigation in relation to the major safety equipment groups. Vehicle failure contributing to an accident is usually related to the following:

1. Defective brakes.
2. Defective lights.
3. Defective steering.
4. Defective tires.
5. Defective wheels.

A specific fault of a vehicle's mechanism not within the general category of safety groups does not generally contribute to accidents, but if found to make such a contribution upon investigation, it would certainly be reported as a vehicle defect.

Road Conditions

These environmental conditions are often found to be contributing causes of accidents. The conditions usually cited by accident investigators as possibly contributing to traffic accidents are generally within the scope of the following categories:

1. Type of road (not divided, divided, number of lanes, access control).
2. Road geometry (straight, curve, level, grade, crest of hill, intersection, offset intersection, railroad crossing, merging lanes, tunnel or bridge).
3. Road condition (dry, wet, icy or snowy).
4. Weather condition (clear, raining, snowing or sleeting, fog or smog).
5. Light condition (daylight, dawn or dusk, darkness).
6. Traffic control (none, traffic signal, stop sign, yield sign, speed reduction, other warning devices).
7. Sight distance (vision obscurements because of road geometry, type of road, or nearby view obstructions).

Investigators may conclude that the presence of one of the above conditions may have contributed meaningfully to the accident. The absence of another road factor may have been a contributor, or some combination of environmental factors might be classed among the multiple causes of a single accident.

Determining Responsibility

The type of driving and walking forbidden by the vehicle code is believed to lead to accidents. Police activity in enforcing such laws has reduced accidents in the areas of enforcement. Such laws spell out speed too fast for conditions, infringements on the substantial right-of-way of another traffic user, and other behavior likely to be listed by a skilled investigator as among driver failures leading to accidents. Modern accident investigators and police officials do not concede that "law violations tend to be the legal and police concept of causes of traffic accidents," but have a firm opinion that within the function of police traffic control is a determination of responsibility in connection with law violation as a contributing circumstance to an accident on the highway. It is vital to on-the-scene enforcement against the accident participant. Police seek for the accident-contributing violation of law for a single act of police enforcement within the scope of driver failure.

Police also report to interested agents of government and vehicle manufacturers the nature of their assignment of responsibility in relation to vehicle defects; they report similarly to traffic and highway engineers their findings on road conditions.

These actions are within the police function, but the primary action is on the enforcement front. For this reason many police departments prepare lists of violations found to contribute to accidents locally and organize their selective enforcement campaigns upon police reports of such violations as contributing to traffic accidents. In California the provisions of the vehicle code and reports of police accident investigations have been collated into the following list of forty-seven violations noted as causing accidents:

1. Exceeding safe speed but not stated limit.
2. Exceeding maximum speed limit.
3. Excessive speed and rear-end collision.
4. Exceeding stated speed limit.
5. Impeding traffic.
6. Wrong side of road—not passing.
7. Changing lanes without safety.
8. Cutting in.
9. Illegal passing on right.
10. Illegal passing without sufficient clearance on intersections, curves, hillcrests.
11. Following too closely.
12. Caution in passing animals.
13. Passing school bus and failing to stop.
14. Violating right-of-way (auto).
15. Improper turning position.
16. Improper starting from parked position.
17. Improper parking.
18. Failed to observe stop sign or flashing signal.
19. Stop-and-go lights.
20. Failure to heed other signs.
21. Failure to stop at railroad crossing.
22. Failure to signal properly; turning without safety.
23. Driving while under influence of intoxicating liquor.
24. Driving while under influence of drugs.
25. Out of control: asleep.
26. Out of control: heart, diabetes, epilepsy, etc.
27. Out of control: self-medication (antihistamines, sleep deterents, sedatives).
28. Loose stock on highway.

29. Striking another animal or fowl.
30. All light violations.
31. All brake violations, except 36 and 44.
32. Mirrors.
33. Defective or dirty windshields or wipers.
34. Unsafe vehicle or other mechanical failure.
35. Whipping trailers, safety chains.
36. Out of control: runaway truck (commercial vehicle or combination over which the driver has lost control of its speed through misuse of brakes or inadequate brakes on any grade).
37. Spilling loads.
38. Unsafe load.
39. Throwing or dropping injurious material on highway.
40. Mountain driving.
41. Crowding or obstructing view of driver, unlawful riding.
42. Inattentive or attention diverted (illegal TV, insects, etc.).
43. Opening door on street side of parked vehicle.
44. Unattended motor vehicle.
45. Violating right-of-way (pedestrian).
46. Pedestrian violations (other than for drinking).
47. Drunk pedestrian.

If the facts of an accident did not support an assignment of one or more of the above violations as a cause of the accident, a note would be made on all records, "No violation indicated."

Classification of Accidents

The investigator must classify an accident in accordance with collision and noncollision grouping, utilizing his determination of the key event for this purpose.

One or more wheels of a vehicle must be off the road for the first classification of running off the road. The shoulder of a highway is considered part of the road if a vehicle could be driven upon the shoulder without bogging down or tipping over. Running off the road is the most common key event in the noncollision types of accidents, but "overturned in the road" and "other noncollision" accidents are common to rural areas.

In the collision accidents there are eight classifications listed. These are collisions with the following objects:

1. Pedestrian.
2. Other motor vehicle.
3. Parked motor vehicle.
4. Train.
5. Bicyclist.
6. Animal.
7. Fixed object.
8. Other object (includes streetcar and animal-drawn vehicle).

In New York City, the classification of "other motor vehicle" collisions were subclassified because remedial action based on engineering studies requires such information. The subclassification of these collisions is as follows:

(a) Head-on.
(b) Head-on left-turn.
(c) Sideswipe—same direction.
(d) Sideswipe—opposing direction.
(e) Sideswipe—parked vehicle.
(f) Right turn.
(g) Rear end.

Lastly, all accidents are classified as *fatal* when a person is killed, as a *critical injury accident* when the personal injury is serious and the victim likely to die, as *serious* when personal injuries are extensive and severe, as *minor* in cases of lesser personal injuries, as *RMA* —Refused Medical Attention—when a participant claims injury but refused medical aid and no diagnosis of injury is available to the police investigator, and as *property damage only* when no one is injured in the accident.

Chapter 13

ACCIDENT INVESTIGATION PROCEDURES

The accident investigator is concerned with drivers and pedestrians involved in accidents, witnesses, physical evidence, vehicle defects, and road and weather conditions. In an accident investigation the assigned police investigator must get to the scene of the accident, administer first aid, make appropriate requests for assistance, direct traffic, interview principals and witnesses, examine and safeguard the scene, collect and preserve evidence, and take appropriate photographs and measurements.

Many years ago, an accident investigator stated in open court that it was standard police procedure to presume that one or more of the participants in an accident were guilty of some vehicle code violation. Today, modern accident investigation procedures start on the presumption that all of the participants are innocent of any wrongdoing. They may have acted unsafely in their driving or walking, but police investigation is concerned with accident reconstruction, not primarily with enforcement. True, police action of a summary nature is often taken after an accident investigation is concluded, but this is a by-product of the procedures used to determine the truth of what happened on the highway at the time of the accident.

An early duty of the accident investigator is to determine if the accident is a hit-and-run case. A prompt radio broadcast of a description of the fleeing car and of possible damage is a standard procedure for apprehending drivers who leave the scene of a crime. The investigator is also expected to assign responsibility for the accident, take police action whenever a violation of the vehicle code is involved in this assignment of responsibility, and gather evidence which will support the essential elements of the vehicle code violation charged by the investigating officer and be relevant and material to the issues of accident causation. This evidence is expected to constitute a *prima facie* case and prove the guilt of the accused person beyond a reasonable doubt in order to combat the presumption of innocence of the defendant in any criminal action.

Investigators should follow the same general procedures in all cases. Of course, fatal and critical injury accidents will probably occupy a larger portion of an investigator's time, but the procedures followed should be nothing more than an extension of the standard procedure used in all cases. It is this methodology of standardizing procedures in all cases that insures a comprehensive investigation in important cases. The investigator becomes familiar with a routine because of its use as a guide in all investigations. Therefore, when it is important that an investigation be complete and comprehensive, it will naturally follow as a result of extending standard procedures.

An investigation must have order. Order can be achieved at the operational level by reviewing all action taken against a prepared master list and maintaining a continuing resumé of the information obtained and the information still to be sought and obtained. Accident investigators usually organize a resumé of this type along the lines of the data required of accident reports (when, where, who, and what) and the opinions and conclusions required in the report of an accident investigation—the how and why of the accident. Others have mimeographed checklists of the classic investigatory query of when, where, who, what, how, and why.

Preparing for the Investigation

Travel time to the accident scene from the point at which the radio notification was received will be shortened if the accident investigator has a thorough knowledge of the main arteries of the area and the obstacles to shortcuts. A knowledge of routes which will be open despite the congestion caused by the accident is an absolute necessity to insure prompt arrival of the investigating unit.

A well-planned route, traveled at normal and legal speeds, insures a prompt arrival without accident to the investigator's car. Accidents can not only maim and kill police officers, but can also be very embarrassing to the commanding officer of an accident investigation squad. Photographs in a local newspaper showing a car bearing the words *Accident Investigation Unit* wrapped around a light pole or a tree not only injures the work of the department in this field, but also lessens the educational value of much of the police unit's enforcement program. Unless directed by the dispatcher to proceed on an emergency basis to assist the injured at the scene, the operator of an accident investigation unit vehicle should drive at a reasonable rate of speed.

Upon arrival at the scene, the investigator should promptly park his police vehicle safely and in a position oriented to the accident. The warning lights of the police vehicle should be used to warn approaching traffic and help to protect the integrity and safety of the accident scene. The white light illumination of the police vehicle's headlights should contribute to the safety aspect of the scene. The parked police vehicle should be in a position to facilitate the use of the police radio and not expose the officer to the hazard of crossing any moving traffic stream in moving from or to the car. The officer should promptly place the necessary flares to alert oncoming traffic, particularly on portions of the roadway not offering a reasonable sight distance for the viewing of the accident by oncoming cars, and isolate the scene, preventing unauthorized persons from entering the scene area, if possible, and preventing those present from altering or destroying evidence.

Service Procedures at Accident Scenes

The servicing of a motor vehicle accident has been systematized. The first police officer at the scene of an accident should proceed as follows:

1. Survey the scene—determine the type of aid and assistance required.
2. Attend to injured person or persons—make them comfortable physically and mentally, keep them warm and assure injured persons that aid is on the way—and administer first-aid procedures. The treatment of shock and prevention of loss of blood are important first-aid procedures in accident cases.
3. Call for, or have a responsible person call for, necessary assistance.
4. Locate operator, or operators, involved and obtain licenses.
5. Request capable volunteers to help safeguard area to prevent fire, secondary accidents, movement of injured by unskilled individuals, and the eradication of skid marks or the destruction of other physical evidence at the scene. Stop or detour traffic, if necessary.
6. Prevent theft of the personal property of accident participants.

If a drunken driver is involved, the officer should place the driver under arrest, keep him/her in custody at all times, and not permit the prisoner to eat or drink any liquid except water until after sobriety and chemical tests have been administered. The officer, when possible, will convey the prisoner to police quarters, or a hospital if injured, and complete tests and other arrest procedures required by local laws and regulations.

If an unlicensed driver is involved, the driver should be held at the scene until the driver's previous record has been ascertained. An arrest should be made when it is justified by the operation of a vehicle while a driver's license is under suspension or revoked, in the event the prisoner has failed to answer two or more previous traffic summonses for moving violations or operating without a license, when proof of identity is insufficient, or when a warrant is on file for the driver.

If a hit-and-run driver is involved in the accident, the officer on the scene should take standard hit-and-run procedures.

The responsibility for the control of traffic, crowd management, and the prevention of thefts at an accident scene originates with the first officer at the scene and is passed on to the ranking superior upon arrival.

The first dilemma that must be resolved by police is whether or not the accident is going to be investigated and photographed without moving the vehicles involved. If photographs are to be taken, the vehicles involved will not be moved unless this is necessary to rescue the injured person or persons involved. However, on major highways at peak traffic periods the amount of traffic suggests prompt movement of the vehicles to prevent congestion leading to secondary accidents. In these cases the integrity of the investigation may be lessened, but immediate gathering of evidence and chalking of the outlines of the road users involved is of some aid in preserving the original positions of the vehicles and important pieces of evidence.

Interviewing Accident Participants and Witnesses

The accident investigator should locate the operator or operators of the vehicles involved as soon as arriving on the scene. The first officer to arrive should do this as he/she pursues the necessary duties of servicing the accident scene. Witnesses should also be located by skilled observation and diplomatic questioning at this time or immediately following the tentative identification of the operator or operators of the vehicles involved.

Officers must make mental notes of the circumstances of locating both principals and witnesses and the identification of the driver of a motor vehicle at the time of the accident. This identification may be vital to the entire investigation and related police action. Officers are usually unable to testify to an observation of a person as being in the driver's seat behind the wheel or close to this position and may require circumstantial evidence or the testimony of other participants and nonparticipant witnesses to make this identification as to the person having operation and control of the vehicle at the time of the accident. Witnesses may be noted as reluctant to identify themselves as observing the accident, anxious to contribute to the police investigation, or as being overprotective of the interest of one of the principals involved in the accident.

Before any questioning, the accident investigator must survey the scene of the accident and call upon his or her own individual expertise for a working theory of the cause of the accident, the contributions of the participants, and the likely violations of law. Usually this is almost a matter of "recognition." A knowledgeable officer develops expectations on the way to an accident scene based upon time of day, day of week, weather conditions, and the intersection or stretch of highway involved. Upon arrival the officer makes a quick survey of the positions of final rest of the traffic units involved, the point of impact, and the approach path of the vehicles. The facts of an accident scene will usually confirm an experienced officer's expectations about 80 percent of the time.

Captain Charles Lehman, Field Commander of New York's Accident Investigation Squad and veteran of twenty years of vehicle homicide investigations, had an accuracy ratio for describing accidents before arrival on the scene that was close to 95 percent. The author rode with Captain Lehman on many Friday and Saturday nights on the highways of New York. While en route to an accident scene this experienced detective would discuss the likely factors contributing to the accident; time after time a view of the scene upon arrival would confirm the circumstances of the accident to be substantially as Captain Lehman had described them. This is an uncanny thing, but many officers develop this ability. Moreover, it puts the officer in a fine position for interviews.

Interviews should be on a one-to-one basis and should be conducted with as much privacy as is possible at an accident scene. They should be structured by the officer along the classic investigative queries of when, where, who, what, how, and why. Officers may stress one or more of these queries when interviewing the various principals and witnesses, but must seek adequate answers on each of these queries.

A structured interview does not mean that the person being interviewed is not given an opportunity to relate what he or she observed in narrative fashion. Narration rather than responding to questioning is the usual form in these interviews. It is the investigator's role to rearrange this information under standard groupings in order to easily compare the statement of one person with information secured from other persons. The closer the questioning is to the moment of impact, the greater the likelihood of an officer's securing a true statement of the events leading up to the accident and the facts of the accident.

These on-the-scene interviews are similar to conversations between a reporter and a news source, or a student and a professor. True, investigators will survey the general intelligence of the person being interviewed, explore the relationships with other participants, avoid any indications of personal animosity toward the person being interviewed, and guard against offending the person. The person being questioned is *not* in custody and is *not* being interrogated, but there is a fact-finding probing by the investigator.

Skilled questioning is required when interviewing an operator after an admission along the lines of "It all happened so fast..." Officers should avoid leading questions when pursuing this avenue of investigation, but they should persist in asking for more detailed answers to the basic question, "Tell me in your own words what you were doing just before impact." If questioning reveals that there was no distraction to the driver, and that he or she had had sufficient sleep within the previous forty-eight hours to exclude the fatigue factor, then the investigating officer's questions should be pointed toward learning whether or not the driver can recall facts about the route taken prior to the accident. Inability to recall turns, signal lights, important intersections, and like road characteristics may indicate automatism. This is particularly true when the same route is traveled day after day by an operator. Automatism creates an environment high in perception delay and is conducive to such driver failures as following too close and ignoring traffic signals.

Leading questions are also out of order when interviewing witnesses. Ask them casually what happened. Let them tell the story without interruption. Only when the story is finished should questions be asked to clarify or supplement the story of the witness.

After this final action, the person being interviewed is asked to sign the investigator's summation of the interview, or to initial the summation. Possibly these individuals may be asked to write their own stories of the accident. The investigator should provide a pen with blue black or black ink, and he can prompt the witness on portions not covered before asking the person making the statement to sign it.

Instruct the witness, "Please put your name and address at the bottom."

A follow-up interview may be required because of conflict between the stories of persons interviewed. Therefore, it is a good policy for officers to work rapidly at an accident scene and conduct interviews which will collect the main elements of the witness's story: (1) what did the witness observe (any of the five senses); (2) was the witness in a position to make such an observation; (3) was the witness capable of making the alleged observation.* Officers should compare the collected data with their own working theory of the accident and quickly move into a follow-up interview when an apparent discrepancy exists, or when there appears to be a likelihood of ascertaining more information. Officers must remember that all witnesses have different frames of reference, varying physical abilities in observation, and an unknown capacity for misrecollection, bias, and interest.

Some very competent accident investigators always conduct a follow-up interview. They use the question, "Is there anything else you may have remembered since we talked that would be important to reconstructing this accident, or is there anything that you have told me that you now wish to change?" This bland query not only may gain valuable information, but it is also an excellent prelude to reviewing the facts as told previously. The officer can truthfully testify to this review question as an opportunity for the person interviewed to add to or change the information given the officer at the accident scene.

In some instances, the original or the follow-up interview must be conducted at a doctor's office or hospital. Officers must make certain prior to any conversation with the principal or witness that the person is physically able to respond to questioning, not semiconscious, in great pain, or under sedation. While most doctors or other medical personnel do not question an officer's duty to conduct interviews, it is good practice to seek permission, as it does indicate to him or her and to any future court review, that a competent medical opinion had been secured as to the rationality of the principal or witness before the interview.

Officers conducting the foregoing interviews at accident scenes are acting within the fact-finding function of police in a general questioning of citizens likely to have information aiding law enforcement, and no

---

*Paul B. Weston, Kenneth M. Wells, and Marlene E. Herloghue, *Criminal Evidence for Police* (Englewood Cliffs, N.J., Prentice-Hall, 1995), pp. 30–32.

special warnings need be given by the officer of the constitutional rights of persons accused of crime prior to or during such interviews.

Interrogation

When the circumstances at an accident scene require the prompt arrest of a principal in the accident for driving while under the influence of intoxicants, it is advisable to warn this person prior to any attempt to secure admissions or a confession regarding the circumstances of intoxication. Current court rules require a person in police custody to be warned of the right to silence and to legal counsel prior to any questioning and that anything the person might say may be used against him or her in court, and procedural rules established for waiving these rights require the waiver to be made "knowingly and intelligently."[*]

In all other arrest cases (such as acting under the authority of a traffic warrant for operating a stolen vehicle or because a violation of the vehicle code has been developed during the investigation), it is likely that the probable cause of the arrest will not develop until the officer has completed general fact-finding questioning while interviewing all persons in a general investigation of the accident, and a special warning and waiver is not necessary to insure the admissibility of the substance of such conversations upon future prosecutions.

PHYSICAL EVIDENCE AT THE SCENE OF ACCIDENTS

Accident investigators thoroughly examine the scene of an accident for physical facts which will contribute to the investigation of the accident. While the information secured from principals and witnesses will generally relate to driver behavior, the examination of an accident scene for physical facts will relate to all three major components of an accident — driver failure, vehicle defects, and road conditions.

The accident should be reconstructed in sequence, with the investigator working from the position of final rest to the approach path of the traffic units involved. The key to accident reconstruction is the two "p's": position and path. The position of all traffic units involved in the accident should be examined and noted. The investigator should examine the position of maximum engagement and point of impact and work

---

[*]Miranda v. Arizona, 384 U.S. 436 (1966).

outward along the paths of the traffic units as they approached the point of initial contact. The investigator also should tie in tire and skid marks and gouges in the roadway with specific vehicles, and *note* items of physical evidence which may have been deposited in the roadway or transferred from one traffic unit to the other during contact. Before moving any of this evidence, photographs should be taken (if warranted by the circumstances of the accident or in accordance with local police unit procedures) and measurements made of the positions of all traffic units and items of evidence.

It is not necessary at this moment to measure the limits of the highway or intersections, view obstructions, or similar physical conditions. The investigator should take as many measurements as may be necessary from points of reference to locate the positions of the traffic units involved and physical evidence discovered.

Highly perishable items of evidence (blood, flesh, dust and dirt, etc.) should be collected, properly marked, tagged, wrapped, and prepared for transport. Other evidence, such as glass from headlight lenses, front grill fragments, and the shoes of pedestrian victims, is collected and preserved and prepared for transport. The examination and search for physical facts is then extended to the vehicles. The investigating officer checks for vehicle defects, particularly to the safety equipment, and for evidence in the area under each vehicle or the pedestrian victim, the underside of each vehicle, and the side of the vehicle that is touching the ground or pavement in the position of final rest. Some officers insist on viewing the under areas of vehicles when tow trucks lift and move them from the scene; they suggest it as a standard procedure. Other policemen believe these examinations and searches may be postponed in order to gain better light conditions or skilled assistance. Officers must use care in postaccident procedures and maintain the required chain of possession to protect the integrity of all collected evidence.

This investigation along the lines of the two "p's" (position and paths) will permit the officer to testify as to the location of the point of impact and other physical signs—road marks, debris, etc. Some courts hold that this is factual testimony, a shorthand of the facts of an accident. It may be necessary for the prosecutor to establish that the training and experience of the police witness in accident investigation is sufficient to qualify the officer to testify concerning his or her observations of these physical facts left at accident scenes after an accident and of their measurement and identification.

Photographs

Photographs should not include bystanders or other officers at the scene, as they distract from the photograph and may cause additional problems at later court appearances. They should be taken by the investigator and processed to maintain their integrity as evidence so the officer-photographer can respond in the affirmative to a question asking if such photos truly portray the accident scene and its details.

Photographs should be taken from the direction each vehicle was traveling, along with at least one picture showing the final rest position of each vehicle or pedestrian involved in the accident. Notes should be made in the accident diagram of the camera's position and its distances from the vehicles when photographed. Any vehicle in the pictures should be included in the diagram.

Officers must use care in composing each picture. Depth of field is a problem for some police officers. In portraying accident scenes, it is important that camera openings offering the most extensive depth of field be used in order to secure an accurate reproduction of the scene. A good general rule is to focus one third of the way into any scene. If vehicles have been moved from the scene, photographs of the damage to these vehicles taken at a garage or parking lot may contribute to the facts of an accident under investigation.

Skid Marks

A mark deposited on the roadway surface due to the sliding of a vehicle's nonrotating tire and wheel over the surface is a *skid mark*. A *side skid mark* (sometimes called a scuff mark) is a roadway marking left by the tire and wheel of a vehicle sliding sideways as a result of a force other than centrifugal force. A *centrifugal skid mark* is a marking on the roadway left by a rotating tire and wheel of a speeding vehicle on a curve when the speed of the vehicle is above the critical speed of the curve, and the centrifugal force entirely or partially overcomes the friction between the mass of the vehicle and its tires and the surface of the roadway.

While extreme acceleration will deposit skid marks on the roadway because of spinning wheels, the skid marks at accident scenes are usually a result of extreme deceleration or radical changes in the direction of the vehicle under study.

The powerful braking systems of modern vehicles cause them to "burn rubber" slightly when the vehicle is braked suddenly and heavily and deposit *impending skid marks* on the road surface.

Impending skid marks are caused by the forward rotation of the wheels being slower than the forward movement of the vehicle. This, incidentally, is the point of maximum effectiveness of a motor vehicle braking system. Then, as the brakes take hold and "lock" the wheels, true skid marks are deposited on the roadway surface. The shadowy beginning of a skid mark along the approach path of the vehicle is the impending skid mark (sometimes referred to as *tire shadow marks*), while the darker markings are the skid mark. The skid mark begins in the impending mark and ends at the point of collision or position of final rest.

The sliding locked wheels of a suddenly decelerated vehicle cause a grinding of the tire against the rough surface of the roadway and a smearing of rubber as this friction creates so much heat that the rubber melts. Minute particles of rubber are darkly visible, clinging to the road surface. The shadow mark before the dark smear of a skid mark is the impending mark of the rolling wheels. Both are easily noted from a position a few feet to either side of the skid mark and about five to ten feet from its point of beginning.

On roads paved with or having repair patches of tar or asphalt, there is a similar smear appearance of the skid mark, but this may be due to the effects of the friction of the sliding tire on the tar or asphalt. On unpaved roads or roadway shoulders, the skid mark is usually a furrow or plowed-up skid mark made by the sliding tire and is similar to the smearing skid mark made in soft material, such as snow, slush, mud, and sand and gravel mixtures, atop paved roadways. On hard, dry, and relatively fine-grain roadways, the skid mark appears as a clean or "erased" surface interspersed with some dark smears as the friction of the sliding tire heats the rubber to a sufficient temperature to deposit distinctive markings. On wet highways, the skid mark is also an erasing of the wet surface, a "squeegee" mark, leaving a dry surface to indicate the skid mark. In some cases the arrival of accident investigation cars is sufficiently prompt to secure pictures of these squeegee marks on wet pavements.

Overlapping skid marks occur when the rear wheels track on top of the front wheel marks. This overlapping must be carefully noted. It is often revealed by a slight offset, a widening and darkening of the skid mark. The investigator must look for the edge lines of the front wheels, as these wheels leave a distinctive mark.

In the conventional automobile with the engine in front, when the brakes are applied there is a transfer of weight forward. This causes the front tires to bow up slightly in the center of the tread, leaving a much heavier deposit of rubber along the outer edges of the skid mark than in the center. This type of marking makes it easy for the investigator to distinguish between front and rear wheel skid marks. He should also look for the end of the rear tire tread marks approximately one wheel-base distance from the end of the marks and trace the front wheel skid marks to their termination at the rear.

Skips occur when a locked and sliding wheel side-hops or bounces over some bump, rut, or other hole in the road. These skips are short, usually from six to thirty-six inches. These skips are included as part of the measurement of a skid mark. Skips are included in measurements of skid marks because friction is directly proportional to the amount of force pressing two surfaces together; when the vehicle comes down after bouncing into the air momentarily, the force between the tire and the surface of the road is greater than normal, thus compensating for the lesser force in operation while the tires are off the ground.

Gaps in skid marks occur when the brakes are released and the wheels unlock momentarily. Gaps are usually longer than eight to ten feet because of the operator's reaction time. Gaps are not included when measuring skid marks.

The investigator should always seek to establish that the skid marks were made by the vehicle under study and the operator's identity established without any doubt. Ask questions directly of the operator: "Were you driving this car?" "Are these your skid marks (indicating)?" "How fast were you driving at the time you put on the brakes?" "Did you jam on your brakes?"

Measurements of skid marks should be made, if possible, while the vehicle is still in its final rest position. This, plus photographs of the vehicle and skid marks, has a high evidential value in court presentations. The investigator's partner or another officer at the scene should note the reading on the tape as skid marks are measured. This officer can then corroborate the investigator's testimony if required in court. These other officers should also have peculiarities of the skid marks pointed out and explained to them so they know something about the wheels making the skid mark and the manner in which it was laid down.

Measure the length of skid marks of each wheel to the nearest half-foot. The skid marks of each wheel are measured even when they are overlapping each other, so long as each wheel's skid mark can be distinguished. If the skid mark is laid on varying kinds of pavement, it is necessary to measure the skid mark separately on each type of pavement. (Coefficients of pavement differ, and unless the length of a skid mark is measured on each surface, it will be impossible to determine the speed of the vehicle from the length of the skid mark.) A curving skid mark is measured around the curve by bending the tape or walking a measuring wheel along the distance of the curve. Pacing should only be used as a last resort, because the inherent element of error present in such methods can be attacked in court by the defense.

To compute the total skid mark, the length of all skid marks are totaled and divided by four. In most cases, there will be four individual skid marks, which accounts for the use of the numeral four as a divisor, but when only two or three individual wheel skid marks can be seen and measured, the same numeral of four is used to divide the total length of all skid marks. While this type of computation favors the operator of the vehicle under study, it is impossible for any investigator to measure something that cannot be seen.

However, it should be noted that a qualified expert witness may reject this four-wheel computing and testify to speed based on the length of single skid marks where the skid marks are in a perfectly straight line. This is because of the fact that if the other three wheels had not been exerting braking effectiveness as great as the one which made the skid mark, despite the lack of discernible skid marks from these wheels, the vehicle would have started to rotate because of the unbalanced physical forces operating on it, and this would have caused a curvature in the skid marks.

The centrifugal skid mark must be related to the critical speed of a highway curve—a constant speed at which the curve can be negotiated safely without "cutting corners." When a vehicle enters a curved section of a roadway at an excessive rate of speed, the centrifugal force is toward the outside of the curve. While the banking of a curve helps speeding cars to hold the road without skipping or side-slipping, the basic formula representing the critical speed of a curve is calculated from the radius of curvature of the highway section. Centrifugal skid marks (and often vehicles leaving the roadway) indicate that the critical speed of the curved section of highway has been exceeded. Accident investigators can measure the radius of these curved sections, but it is an involved and time-consuming process and is not often the subject of testimony by police witnesses upon the trial of offenders. Officers can testify, however, to their own knowledge of the speed limit for the curve as set by the highway department. Vehicle speeds are usually restricted at bad curves, and the limit is below the critical speed of the curve. Courts will recognize the fact that a car leaving a centrifugal skid mark on such a curve, or leaving the roadway within its curvature, has exceeded the specific speed limit by at least ten miles or more.

Some accidents involve centrifugal skid marks where there is no curvature in the road, but the vehicle has exceeded the critical speed for the curve it was executing (U-turn, right turn, etc.). In these situations, measurements along the chord of the arc of the skid mark form the basis for a mathematical determination of the minimum speed of the vehicle.

Test Skids

The drag factor or slipperiness of a road's surface must be known before speed can be calculated from skid marks. This friction is usually represented by a decimal less than 1.00 in computing speed from skid marks and indicates the friction drag on the sliding tires of a car's wheels locked in a panic stop. This drag factor is developed from the test skids, as these skids inform the investigator of the stopping distance of a car decelerating from a known speed. The simplest method is to make test skids on the same roadway and slope and in the same direction of travel of the car as when it skidded in the accident. All variables are removed from computing this drag factor when this method is used. Otherwise the grade of the roadway must be computed and worked into the formula.

When the vehicle which has made the skid marks being studied can be driven, it is used for test skids. The first step is to determine the accuracy of this vehicle's speedometer. Police department vehicles have calibrated speedometers and are utilized in this speedometer testing. The investigating officer should explain the testing procedure to the involved operator. The police vehicle will be driven at a low speed by another officer, and the involved operator will follow in the car being tested, with the investigator driving. The policeman operating the police vehicle will sound his horn when his speedometer reads 25 mph, and he will maintain that speed; the investigating officer will note the speed being recorded at this time on the car being tested and ask the possible defendant to also note it. He will then touch his horn and signal the police car that the test is over. The speed recorded on the possible defendant's vehicle will be the speed used when test skids are made with the vehicle. It represents a true speed of 25 mph. Generally, at least three test skids are made and the lowest value obtained used in determining the coefficient of friction.

Since friction is in direct proportion to the force pressing the two sliding surfaces together, then the coefficient of friction can also be measured using a vehicle other than the one which made the original skid marks, if, as is often the case, that vehicle is not in a drivable condition after the accident. The relative weight of the vehicle makes no difference, as the weight factor cancels out once the wheels have been locked and the vehicle is sliding. It is often more practical to make tests for the coefficient of friction using a police vehicle with a calibrated speedometer; the results obtained from this type of test are just as valid as those obtained from a test with the vehicle involved in the accident.

Speed from Skid Marks

A formula based on a basic principle of physics (any object or body in motion has energy because of its motion) permits an accurate estimate of speed from skid marks. The work needed to stop a vehicle's sliding on a pavement depends on the skid resistance of the pavement (coefficient of friction). To create this energy the car must have traveled at a certain speed, so when this energy is measured the speed of the car is revealed.

The first step in this speed determination is to determine the coefficient of friction from the test skid data. In the formula for determining the coefficient of friction, V stands for the speed (velocity) of the vehicle in miles per hour when the test skid was made, S the distance in feet the car slides in coming to a stop (usually the total length of all skid marks divided by four), and f represents the coefficient of friction. This formula is written as $f = \dfrac{V^2}{30S}$

The figure 30 in the above formula is a necessary constant and conversion factor, as speed is given in miles per hour and the distance traveled in feet. If the test speed was 25 mph and the average skid mark length 28.4 ft. (total skid mark distance divided by four), the formula $f = \dfrac{V^2}{30\ S}$ will give the coefficient of friction as 0.73.

$$f = \frac{V^2}{30\,S} = \frac{(25)^2}{(30)(28.4)} = \frac{625}{852} = .73$$

$$f = .73$$

The formula for finding the initial speed of a vehicle from the coefficient of friction and the length of skid marks is obtained by rearranging the above formula as follows:

$$f = \frac{V^2}{30\,S}$$

$$30Sf = V^2$$
$$V = \sqrt{30fS}$$

Using the value f = 0.73 found above from the test skid and an average skid mark length of 121 ft. the *minimum* initial speed of the accident vehicle is calculated as follows:

$$V = \sqrt{30fS}$$
$$= \sqrt{30 \times 0.73 \times 121}$$
$$= \sqrt{2650}$$
$$= 51.4 \text{ mph}$$

Nomographs against which a straight-edged ruler can be placed may be used to check the officer's calculations. These nomographs have a scale showing the skid distance in feet on the left, a speed scale in the center, and a coefficient of friction scale on the right. When the straight edge of the ruler is placed on the distance of the skid in feet on the left and the coefficient of friction on the right, then the speed can be read at the point where the ruler intersects the speed scale in the center of the page.

These estimates of speed from skid marks are helpful to the accident investigator in assigning responsibility for an accident and in isolating its causes. They indicate to the officer the minimum speed of the vehicle before the stopping action began. The speed is only good to two significant figures because the constant (30) and the coefficient of friction are only two-digit figures.

Police action based solely on estimating speed from skid marks usually involves the investigator in qualifying as an expert witness in this specific field. A court will require the officer to show a working knowledge of the fundamental laws of motion and energy, particularly that branch of physics described as *mechanics*. Extensive accident investigation experience which will show knowledge and skill in locating, identifying, and measuring skid marks, plus a high school course in algebra and physics, is usually the minimum requirement for qualifying as a skid mark expert, and many courts seek college-level training in physics unless the officer can show attendance at above average police training schools specializing in accident investigation. If the officer cannot qualify as an expert in this field, he/she is not allowed to testify as to an estimate of the speed of a vehicle based on its skid marks.

Brake Tests

The brakes of a car can be tested when the test skids are made. If the brakes are inadequate, the operator should be advised that an attempt to demonstrate their adequacy would be allowed.

In most states a vehicle traveling 20 mph must stop within the following *minimum* distance:

1. Two-wheel brakes—foot pedal: vehicle should stop within 45 ft.
2. Four-wheel brakes—foot pedal: vehicle should stop within 30 ft.
3. Hand brakes: vehicle should stop within 75 ft.

Brake tests should not be conducted when the road surface is wet. Tests on wet surfaces may result in personal injuries to bystanders or others concerned in the tests. The vehicle should be examined to ascertain if it complies with legal safety requirements and whether its braking system is in operating order. If the vehicle is found to have less than a one-third pedal reserve, then it should be driven to a garage and tested. While this latter procedure may not withstand court tests, it is within the public interest to reveal persons operating cars with inadequate brakes by prompt police action. The failure to make brake tests on wet pavements puts the police unit in the position of doing nothing. It is far better to report that an examination has been made, and when it appears likely that the brakes are inadequate, then tests are conducted in a dry area.

Brake tests should be conducted on level ground, the common rule being that if a vehicle does not roll when the brakes are released, then the roadway is level and the test may be conducted.

Decelerometers are devices which hold their readings and indicate on a clocklike face the braking efficiency of the car being tested. All decelerometers used in the field should be checked against a master decelerometer, which in turn should be certified for accuracy by the U.S. Bureau of Standards. These devices hold a deceleration reading and indicate braking efficiency. They are small and can be placed on the floor of a car.

ENFORCEMENT ACTION

Enforcement action is a primary objective of accident investigation. The effectiveness of the traffic control program can hardly be criticized when police action shortly after an accident is directed at the person causing the accident. Public knowledge that summary police action will usually follow a motor vehicle accident will be a strong deterrent to hazardous driving habits.

Public knowledge that police action is being taken against operators causing accidents minimizes the commonly held belief that police are doing little or nothing to protect the public from such accidents.

Chapter 14

THE TRAFFIC ACCIDENT REPORT

The basic imperative of writing a traffic accident report is to tell the story of an event, a happening. Drawing a sketch (diagram) is a graphic representation of what happened; writing the narrative portion of a traffic accident report is a words-in-action detailing of the event.

The statewide form in general use for this reporting is full of boxes requiring the reporting officer to respond to queries so that the report has an orderly array of information about the event. The arraying of data on these reports fosters compiling and analysis useful to police traffic control managers.

Sketching the Scene

Sketching should begin promptly when the essential work of interviewing principals and witnesses and collecting data on the physical facts of an accident has been completed. It is usually integrated with the act of measuring for reference points and localizing the physical conditions at the accident scene. A rough sketch should be made before the removal of evidence or the traffic units involved in the accident. If any evidence or a vehicle must be moved because of the exigencies of police service, the exact location of the item removed should be chalked upon the pavement at the scene.

Basic symbols should be used to describe and identify items shown in the sketch, particularly the paths of the traffic unit(s) involved, point(s) of impact, and position(s) of final rest. Measurements must be accurate and all traffic units clearly identified. In addition, sketches of the accident scene require a compass direction to orient the sketch geographically, data on time, location and weather, and the identification and location of important items of evidence by a descriptive symbol and measurements to at least two reference points. Rectangular coordinates, measurements made at right angles to the nearest curb, crosswalk, building line or highway shoulder, or triangulation from two fixed and identifiable objects not likely to be removed from the accident scene are the acceptable methods of locating important objects on sketches of accident scenes.

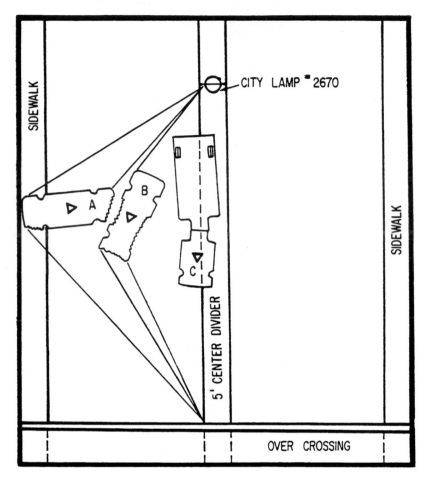

Figure 15-A. A schematic representation of an accident scene. Measured distances in the diagram should be inserted along all reference lines.

Items concerning either the road users involved or the physical characteristics of the roadway which do not aid in reproducing the accident should not be shown in a sketch. An investigator usually puts too much detail into a sketch. The less explaining an officer has to do in court concerning the scene and the diagram, the clearer the officer's testimony is likely to be and the less chance of error and confusion (See Figures 15 and 16).

In the preparation of these sketches many officers use a standard

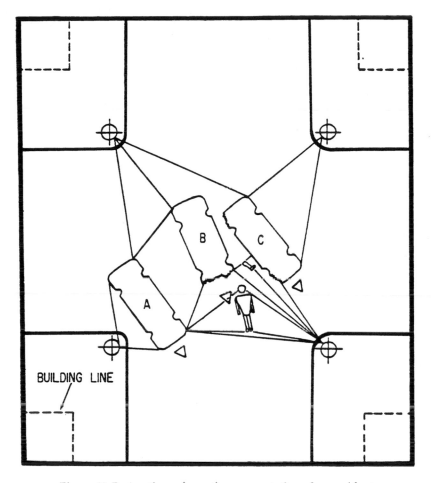

Figure 15-B. Another schematic representation of an accident.

template with cutouts of various vehicles, traffic devices, and like symbols. Whether a sketch is large or small, it is a diagram of what happened at the scene of the accident.

Written Reports

Since a sketch of an accident scene and the photographs of an accident graphically reproduce scene conditions, a written report must correspond with such evidence. All too often a written report disagrees with photographs or the scene sketch, or both. This is particularly true of the narrative portion of a report. This story of the accident must be aligned with the facts indicated in scene photos or in accident diagrams.

The narrative should not repeat information *clearly* indicated in the sketch or adequately described elsewhere, except when necessary to explain the occurrence of the collision.

The data disclosed by the reporting officer's investigation should be reported under the following major headings:

a. **Facts:** Only those facts not indicated in sketch or elsewhere in the collision report are to be entered here. Facts include, but are not limited to, the following:

   (1) *Time* call was received and time of arrival.

   (2) *Description of scene,* including such items as roadway surface, number of lanes, fixed objects, as necessary.

   (3) *Vehicle* location, damage, defects, and how these defects were detected. Repeat the sequence for all vehicles as applicable.

   (4) *Physical evidence* such as skid marks, roadway gouges, debris, vehicle parts, disposition of evidence.

   (5) *Other* factual and pertinent information; for example, driver's license restrictions, injuries, tests administered, the number of photographs taken of the scene, and the name and phone number of the photographer if other than an officer.

b. **Statements:** Statements need not be verbatim. The reporting officer should record the substance of the statement, eliminating unnecessary detail and arranging the explanation in a logical, meaningful order. In the event written statements are received, write "statements attached" in the narrative.

c. **Opinions and Conclusions:** The purpose of this section is to explain the occurrence of the collision. Avoid the use of stilted or formal phrases. The words "it is my opinion" need never be used, as the use of an "opinion" and "conclusions" headings clearly indicates that the statement is the officer's opinion and his conclusions. The term "as stated by Party No _____" should be used only when the statement adequately summarizes the collision.

   (1) The reporting officer should give his opinion, based on his full investigation, of the occurrences that took place and explain how the collision happened in his own words. He should also state his opinion of the point of impact and briefly explain factors which support his opinion.

   (2) Vehicle Code violations should be entered, along with an

explanation of the evidence upon which the officer's opinion is based. When prosecution is anticipated and the elements of the offense are not documented in another report, such as an arrest or intoxication report, the source of proof to be used for establishing the elements of the offense should be entered here. For example, "Party No. 1, Mr. Jones, was in violation of 22450 V.C., failure to stop at a stop sign, based upon statements of witnesses, J. Smith (driving) and R. Wilson (failure to stop), and skid marks beginning west of limit line, continuing east across limit line into the intersection to the point of rest of Vehicle No. 1. (See Photos)."

d. **Recommendations:** The reporting officer may recommend necessary follow-up action by another person or agency. If the reporting officer has no recommendations, the word "none" should be written after inserting this heading.

Uniform Symbols—Sketching

To assure uniformity in description and interpretation, the basic symbols with universal meaning throughout the state should be used for all collision sketching. See Figures 16-A and 16-B for these symbols and examples of their use. Note that the small circle indicates the initial point of impact (POI). More than one point of impact may be shown on a sketch. Where additional points of impact are required, number consecutively—beginning with the initial POI. Also note: Paths of vehicles, before and after point(s) of impact, are indicated by solid lines; continue solid lines to the *point of rest* for each involved vehicle. Place an arrow head at each POI to indicate general direction and number the solid lines as necessary to identify vehicles. Rollovers are indicated by spiraling these solid lines. Paths of pedestrians or animals are indicated by dashed lines. When more detail is required, a larger sketch may be drawn.

Sketch and Narrative Examples

Following are several examples of acceptable sketches and narratives for collision reports.

Sketch: See Figure 17.

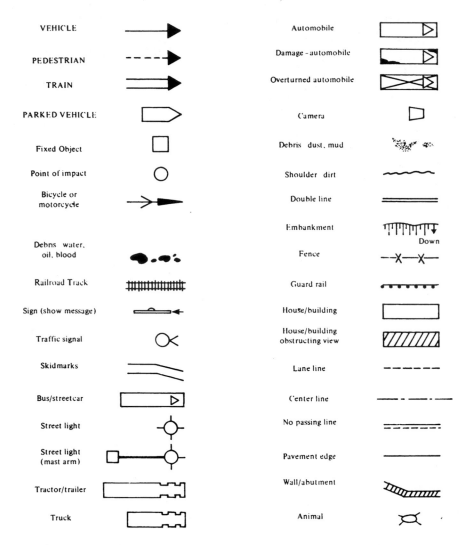

VEHICLE	Automobile
PEDESTRIAN	Damage - automobile
TRAIN	Overturned automobile
PARKED VEHICLE	Camera
Fixed Object	Debris dust, mud
Point of impact	Shoulder dirt
Bicycle or motorcycle	Double line
	Embankment Down
Debris water, oil, blood	Fence
Railroad Track	Guard rail
Sign (show message)	House/building
Traffic signal	House/building obstructing view
Skidmarks	Lane line
Bus/streetcar	Center line
Street light	No passing line
Street light (mast arm)	Pavement edge
Tractor/trailer	Wall/abutment
Truck	Animal

Figure 16-A. Basic symbols: reporting parties involved and physical characterstics of accident scene in collision report sketches.

Narrative: V-3 was slowing in traffic N/B in I-50 in the N/B-1 lane when it was struck from behind by V-2. After striking V-3, V-2 was struck from behind by V-1.

Sketch: See Figure 17.

Narrative: V-1 was E/B on Jenkins Dr. in the E-1 lane and struck V-2 which was S/B on Main St. After impact both vehicles went out of control. V-2 rolled over twice before coming to rest.

Sketch: See Figure 17.

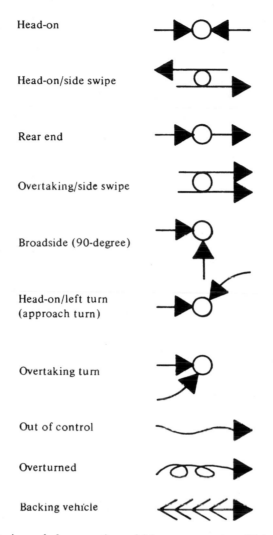

Head-on

Head-on/side swipe

Rear end

Overtaking/side swipe

Broadside (90-degree)

Head-on/left turn
(approach turn)

Overtaking turn

Out of control

Overturned

Backing vehicle

Figure 16-B. Basic symbols: reporting vehicle movement in collision report sketches.

Narrative: V-1 was S/B on Bay Ave. in the S-1 lane and made a left turn on Elm St. striking V-2 which was parked facing E/B on Wells St. After impact V-1 went out of control and struck a fire hydrant on the north side of Wells St.

As illustrated, the arrow in the circle on each segment of the drawing points North.

Most officers use a template with cutouts available commercially. Template use makes these sketches/diagrams neater than freehand drawing and helps in drawing to scale. If vehicles or objects were moved from

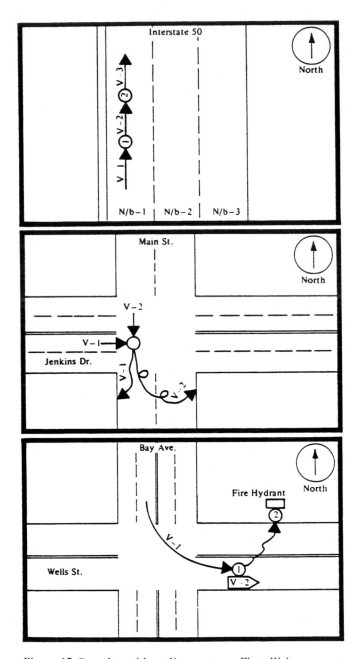

Figure 17. Sample accident diagrams—traffic collision report.

their point of rest before the arrival of the reporting officer, they need not be shown in the sketch/diagram.*

Traffic Accident Report — Uniform Data

To gain uniformity in statewide reporting of traffic accidents, all officers must use a standardized form in reporting these events. Illustrated is California's, but nationwide all of these forms seek the same information in the same order — vital to coding and analysis. Of course, the diagram and narrative sections are informational, but for gathering data for insertion into and retrieval from a records system, they are only supplementary to "boxed" information.

The following comment on the how-to of preparing this form is in numbered paragraphs keyed to the numbers shown on this form in Figures 18-A and 18-B.

1. *Special Conditions:* This box is used to note the following conditions requiring special handling:
   a. Fatal.
   b. Preliminary.
   c. Private property.
   d. "Counter Report." (This entry applies to a late report of a property-damage-only collision reported by an involved party at a police facility or California Highway Patrol office.)
   e. Explosives.
   f. Hazardous materials.
   g. School bus:
      (1) Enter the *category* and *class* of the school bus.
          (a) The school bus category is determined by the identification required to be displayed on each side of the bus. The school bus category entered in the "Special Conditions" box will be either "Public School Bus," "Private School Bus," or "Contractor School Bus."
          (b) The school bus class is determined by the bus design and is entered in the "Special Conditions" box following the school bus category; for example, "Contractor School Bus 2."
          (c) The number of pupils in the bus at the time of the

---

* ——, *Collision Investigation Manual* (Sacramento, California, California Highway Patrol, 1992), p. 4–59.

TRAFFIC COLLISION REPORT   DEPARTMENT OF CALIFORNIA HIGHWAY PATROL   PAGE 9 OF ___

SPECIAL CONDITIONS	NO. INJ.	H & R FELONY	CITY	JUDICIAL DISTRICT	No.
1	2	☐ 3	4	5	10
	NO. KILLED	H & R MISD ☐	COUNTY 6	REPORTING DISTRICT 7	BEAT 8

LOCATION

COLLISION OCCURRED ON 11	MO. DAY YR. 14	TIME(2400) 15	CH NO 16	OFFICER I.D. 17

☐ AT INTERSECTION WITH
☐ OR: ___ FEET/MILES ___ OF

INJURY, FATAL OR TOW AWAY 18 ☐ YES ☐ NO   STATE HWY 19 ☐ YES ☐ NO

PARTY 1

☐ DRIVER	NAME (FIRST, MIDDLE, LAST) 21	STREET ADDRESS 22

DRIVER'S LICENSE NO. 23	STATE	BIRTHDATE MO. DAY YR. 24	SEX 25	RACE 26	CITY	STATE	PHONE

☐ PEDES-TRIAN

VEHICLE YR. 27	MAKE 28	LICENSE NO. 29	STATE	OWNER'S NAME ☐ SAME AS DRIVER 30

☐ PARKED VEH.

DIRECTION OF 31	ON/ACROSS (STREET OR HIGHWAY)	OWNER'S ADDRESS ☐ SAME AS DRIVER

☐ BI-CYCLIST

☐ OTHER

SPEED LIMIT 32	DISPOSITION OF VEHICLE 33	☐ BY DRIVER	ON ORDERS OF 34	VEHICLE DAMAGE EXTENT ☐ MINOR ☐ MOD. ☐ MAJOR ☐ TOTAL	LOCATION 35	VIOLATION CHARGED 1 ___ 36 2 ___

PARTY 2

☐ DRIVER	NAME (FIRST, MIDDLE, LAST)	STREET ADDRESS

DRIVER'S LICENSE NO.	STATE	BIRTHDATE MO. DAY YR.	SEX	RACE	CITY	STATE	PHONE

☐ PEDES-TRIAN

VEHICLE YR.	MAKE	LICENSE NO.	STATE	OWNER'S NAME ☐ SAME AS DRIVER

☐ PARKED VEH.

DIRECTION OF	ON/ACROSS (STREET OR HIGHWAY)	OWNER'S ADDRESS ☐ SAME AS DRIVER

☐ BI-CYCLIST

☐ OTHER

SPEED LIMIT	DISPOSITION OF VEHICLE	☐ BY DRIVER	ON ORDERS OF	VEHICLE DAMAGE EXTENT ☐ MINOR ☐ MOD. ☐ MAJOR ☐ TOTAL	LOCATION	VIOLATION CHARGED 1 ___ 2 ___

PROPERTY

DESCRIPTION OF DAMAGE 38

OWNER'S NAME 39	ADDRESS	NOTIFIED 39A ☐ YES ☐ NO

INJURED/WITNESS

WITNESS ONLY	AGE	SEX	EXTENT OF INJURY				INJURED WAS (check one)					IN VEH. NUMBER
			FATAL INJURY	SEVERE WOUND DISTORTED MEMBER	OTHER VISIBLE INJURIES	COMPLAINT OF PAIN	DRIVER	PASS.	PED.	BI-CYCLIST	OTHER	
☐ 40	41	42	☐	☐	☐	☐	☐	☐	☐	☐	☐	45

NAME 46   43   PHONE 44

ADDRESS 47   TAKEN TO (INJURED ONLY)

☐		☐	☐	☐	☐	☐	☐	☐	☐	☐

NAME   PHONE

ADDRESS   TAKEN TO (INJURED ONLY) 48

49

☐		☐	☐	☐	☐	☐	☐	☐	☐	☐

NAME   PHONE

ADDRESS   TAKEN TO (INJURED ONLY)

SKETCH 50   (INDICATE NORTH)   MISCELLANEOUS 51

VEHICLE TYPE			
PARTY 1		PARTY 2	

ROAD TYPE
A CONVENTIONAL, ONE WAY
B CONVENTIONAL, TWO WAY
C EXPRESSWAY
D FREEWAY
E OTHER (EXPLAIN IN NARRATIVE)

555 (REV. 11-71)   57698 - 456 555 Rev 11-71 500M OSP

No.

PAGE _____

COLLISION NARRATIVE
52

63

PRIMARY COLLISION FACTOR	RIGHT OF WAY CONTROL	1	2	3	4	TYPE OF VEHICLE	1	2	3	4	MOVEMENT PRECEDING COLLISION
A VC SECTION VIOLATION	A CONTROLS FUNCTIONING					A PASSENGER CAR (INCLUDES STATION WAGON)					A STOPPED
B OTHER IMPROPER DRIVING*	B CONTROLS NOT FUNCTIONING					B PASSENGER CAR W/TRAILER					B PROCEEDING STRAIGHT
C OTHER THAN DRIVER*	C CONTROLS OBSCURED					C MOTORCYCLE/SCOOTER					C RAN OFF ROAD
D UNKNOWN	D NO CONTROLS PRESENT					D PICKUP OR PANEL TRUCK					D MAKING RIGHT TURN
WEATHER	TYPE OF COLLISION					E PICKUP OR PANEL TRUCK W/TRAILER					E MAKING LEFT TURN
A CLEAR	A HEAD-ON					F TRUCK OR TRUCK TRACTOR					F MAKING U TURN
B CLOUDY	B SIDESWIPE					G TRUCK OR TRUCK TRACTOR W/TRAILER(S)					G BACKING
C RAINING	C REAR END					H SCHOOL BUS					H SLOWING - STOPPING
D SNOWING	D BROADSIDE					I OTHER BUS					I PASSING OTHER VEHICLE
E FOG	E HIT OBJECT					J EMERGENCY VEHICLE					J CHANGING LANES
F OTHER	F OVERTURNED					K HIGHWAY CONSTRUCTION EQUIPMENT					K PARKING MANEUVER
LIGHTING	G AUTO/PEDESTRIAN					L BICYCLE					L ENTERING TRAFFIC FROM SHOULDER, MED- IAN, PARKING STRIP OR PRIVATE DRIVE
A DAYLIGHT	H OTHER					M OTHER					
B DUSK - DAWN	MOTOR VEHICLE INVOLVED WITH										M OTHER UNSAFE TURNING
C DARK - STREET LIGHTS	A NON-COLLISION										N CROSSED INTO OPPOSING LANE
D DARK - NO STREET LIGHTS	B PEDESTRIAN	1	2	3	4	OTHER ASSOCIATED FACTOR (MARK ONE TO THREE ITEMS)					O PARKED
E DARK - STREET LIGHTS NOT FUNCTIONING	C OTHER MOTOR VEHICLE					A VC SECTION VIOLATION					P MERGING
ROADWAY SURFACE	D MOTOR VEHICLE ON OTHER ROADWAY					B VC SECTION VIOLATION					Q TRAVELING WRONG WAY*
A DRY	E PARKED MOTOR VEHICLE					C VC SECTION VIOLATION					R OTHER
B WET	F TRAIN					D VC SECTION VIOLATION					
C SNOWY - ICY	G BICYCLE					E VISION OBSCUREMENTS	1	2	3	4	SOBRIETY - DRUG - PHYSICAL (MARK ONE TO THREE ITEMS)
D SLIPPERY (MUDDY, OILY, ETC.)	H ANIMAL					F INATTENTION					A HAD NOT BEEN DRINKING
ROADWAY CONDITIONS (MARK ONE TO THREE ITEMS)	I FIXED OBJECT					G STOP & GO TRAFFIC					B HBD - UNDER INFLUENCE
A HOLES, DEEP RUTS	J OTHER OBJECT					H ENTERING/LEAVING RAMP					C HBD - NOT UNDER INFLUENCE
B LOOSE MATERIAL ON ROADWAY	K OTHER					I PREVIOUS COLLISION					D HBD - IMPAIRMENT UNKNOWN*
C OBSTRUCTION ON ROADWAY	PEDESTRIAN'S ACTION					J UNFAMILIAR WITH ROAD					E UNDER DRUG INFLUENCE
D CONSTRUCTION-REPAIR ZONE	A NO PEDESTRIAN INVOLVED					K DEFECTIVE VEHICLE EQUIPMENT					F OTHER PHYSICAL IMPAIRMENT*
E REDUCED ROADWAY WIDTH	B CROSSING IN CROSSWALK AT INTERSECTION					L UNINVOLVED VEHICLE					G IMPAIRMENT NOT KNOWN
F FLOODED	C CROSSING IN CROSSWALK - NOT AT INTERSECTION					M OTHER*					H NOT APPLICABLE
G OTHER	D CROSSING - NOT IN CROSSWALK					N NONE APPARENT					
H NO UNUSUAL CONDITIONS	E IN ROAD - INCLUDES SHOULDER										
	F NOT IN ROAD										
INVESTIGATED BY 54	G APPROACHING/LEAVING SCHOOL BUS										
	I.D. NUMBER	INVESTIGATED BY 54-a						I.D. NUMBER			REVIEWED BY 55
*EXPLAIN IN NARRATIVE											

Figure 18-A and 18-B. Traffic accident report form. Numbers have been inserted as a guide to instructions for preparing this form. Form design and content of instructions have been planned to serve a statewide (California) computerized traffic records system.

collision shall be recorded in narrative portion of the report (#52).

2. *Number of People Injured Killed:* Enter the total number of people injured or killed as a result of the collision. These totals must be consistent with the number of victims entered in the "Injured/Witnesses" category.

3. *Hit-and-Run Felony or Hit-and-Run Misdemeanor:* Mark an "X" in the applicable box when the facts and evidence indicate that a felony or a misdemeanor hit-and-run violation was committed. Leave blank if a hit-and-run violation is not involved.

4. *City:* Enter the name of the city in which the collision occurred if the city name is not preprinted in the form heading.

5. *Judicial District:* Enter the name of the applicable municipal or justice court.

6. *County:* Enter the name of the county in which the collision occurred.

7. *Reporting District:* Enter, as applicable, the number of the "District," "Division," or other geographical reporting area above the level of a beat.

8. *Beat:* Enter the appropriate beat number, if applicable.

9. *"Page 2 of 2:'* Each side of Forms 555 and 556* is a separate page. For example, an entry of "Page 1 of 2" on the Form 555 face page would indicate that the collision report consists of a single Form 555. A second Form 555 face page used for a collision with more than two involved parties need only have the page number entered here. Entry of total pages is not necessary on the second Form 555. If both sides of Forms 555 and 556 are used, a proper entry would be "Page 1 of 4."

10. *Number:* Enter the case number assigned to the collision. On a second or subsequent Form 555 face page used, no other heading information, except page number, is required.

11. *Collision Occurred On:* Enter the number of the highway. Use only commonly accepted abbreviations preceding the number (for example, United States Highway: U.S., and State Route: S.R.). If not numbered or named, describe the location of the highway. Use an address to identify location of collisions occurring on private property. In addition,

a. When a collision occurs within an intersection, enter the

---

*Numbers of California's report form.

number of the highway with the higher classification. Highway classifications ranked in descending order are as follows:

(1) Interstate System.

(2) Other highways with full control of access, such as freeways and parkways not in the Interstate System.

(3) Other U.S. numbered routes.

(4) Other State numbered routes.

(5) Other major arterials which are usually city streets or county highways for which cross traffic is required to stop.

(6) County roads.

(7) Local streets.

(8) All other highways which do not fall into the above categories, such as alleys and private roads open to the public for purposes of vehicular travel.

b. Collisions occurring within intersections on highways of the same classification shall be assigned to that highway upon which the party most at fault was traveling.

c. Following a county road, city street, alley name, or number; enter "CR" for county road or "CS" for city street.

d. For private property collisions, write out the location, such as private driveway, parking lot.

e. Identify unnamed access or frontage roads adjacent to highways by their direction from the highway; for example, I-80, South frontage road.

f. Identify collisions occurring on unnamed alleys by their direction from a parallel named street. For example, "alley north of 'B' street," or "alley east of 14th Avenue."

g. Collisions occurring on freeway ramps shall be entered in accordance with the following examples:

(1) I-80 E/B off ramp to SR-111 N/B.

(2) Imperial Avenue S/B on ramp to I-80 E/B.

h. When a vehicle runs off the road and the first injury or damage-producing event in the collision occurs off the road, the proper entry in this "Location" section is the point where the vehicle left the road. (The location of injury and/or damage will be described in the body of the report.) For all other collisions the location of the "first event" shall be entered, i.e. the first injury or damage-producing event listed in the

"Motor Vehicle Involved With" category on the reverse side of Form 555.

    i. Milepost reference may be entered following the highway name or number if sufficient space exists. Record all information on the milepost marker reading from the top down.

12. *At Intersection With:* Mark an "X" in this box and enter the route number or name of the intersecting highway, alley, etc., to the right of this box, if the collision occurs within an intersection.

13. *Or*   *Feet Miles* _____ *Of:* When the collision does *not* occur at an intersection, mark an "X" in this box, and to the right of the box enter the distance and direction from the nearest permanent reference point, such as an intersecting street, overcrossing, county line. If such a reference point is not present within a reasonable distance, enter the distance and direction from the nearest commonly known identifiable landmark. Also,

    a. If the collision occurs at a railroad crossing, mark this box and enter the distance and direction from the nearest permanent reference point. Enter the P.U.C. grade crossing number following the name of the reference point. Enter the name of the railroad right-of-way property owner in the narrative (Southern Pacific, Western Pacific, etc.).

    b. Line out "Feet" or "Miles," whichever is not applicable. Selective enforcement and highway design improvements are dependent upon identification of the exact collision location. Therefore, it is most important that distances to permanent reference points be measured and not estimated.

    c. For nonintersection collisions where tape measurement or pacing is not practical due to the distance from a reference point, the reporting officer should drive to the nearest intersecting street, road structure, etc., or commonly known identifiable landmark, and calculate the distance using the patrol vehicle odometer. (Line out "feet" and enter the distance in miles and/or tenths of miles; "1.7 miles" or "0.3 miles" would be proper entries).

    d. Enter the distance and direction from the nearest milepost marker, if available, recording information on the marker reading from the top down. For example, 150-E-50 SAC 5[10], indicates that the collision occurred 150 feet east (using route destination alignment, not compass direction) from the milepost 50 SAC 5^{10}.

14. ***Date:*** Enter the numeric month, day, and year (for example, 3/12/73). For collisions where the exact date cannot be determined, such as hit-and-run cases, the reporting officer should make entry based upon his best judgment. Do not leave this space blank.

15. ***Time:*** Enter the time that the collision occurred using international time, except that 2359 will be used instead of 2400 to be compatible with data processing procedures of data-using agencies. For example, use 2359 for a collision occurring exactly at midnight, 0015 for fifteen minutes after midnight, etc. Do not leave this space blank. If the exact time cannot be determined, the reporting officer should make a single time entry based upon his or her best judgment.

16. ***CII Number:*** Enter the four (4) digit code number assigned by the Department of Justice. This is the unique number for each jurisdiction contained in the NCIC directory.

17. ***Officer I.D.:*** Enter the badge or identification number of the reporting officer (one only).

NOTE: Date, Time, CII Number, and officer I.D. must be completed, as they comprise the field-generated collision report number which is used to identify the collision report in the statewide records system computer files. When an involved party reports a collision, an officer I.D. number (desk officer, accident investigation officer, sergeant, etc.) *must be* entered on the Form 555 face page to complete the Collision Report number. An officer's name should not, in this case, be entered in the "Investigated By" space on the lower reverse of Form 555.

18. ***Injury, Fatal, or Tow Away:***
   a. Mark an "X" in the "Yes" box when the collision results in any of the following:
      (1) A fatality.
      (2) An injury.
      (3) Damage to a motor vehicle to the extent that it cannot be driven or, in the case of trailers, towed from the scene of the collision in the usual manner after simple repairs (*excludes* headlamp or taillight damage which would make night driving hazardous, but would not

affect daytime driving and vehicles towed away only because the driver is incapacitated.)

b. Mark an "X" in the "No" box when the collision results in property damage only and vehicle damage is not disabling, that is, all vehicles can be driven from the scene under their own power.

19. *State Highway:* Mark an "X" in the appropriate box to indicate whether or not the collision occurred on or was "associated with" a state highway.

a. To be "associated with" a state highway, the collision location is on other than a state highway, but in proximity to a state highway. For example, collisions which occur near an over-crossing, on a frontage road, etc., generally would be considered "associated with" such highway.

b. To be "associated with" a state highway is a determination that must be made by the officer after giving consideration to such factors as the distance of the collision from the state highway and movement of involved parties prior to the collision. For example, was the collision within a reasonable distance from a state highway and was an involved party preparing to enter a state highway or had an involved party just left a state highway, etc.?

c. The Division of Highways will use this information in their collision location files to identify high collision-frequency locations on or near state highways.

20. *Involved Party Category (Party 1):* Mark an "X" in the box which best describes the involved party: driver, pedestrian, parked vehicle, or bicyclist. If the "Other" box is marked, identify the "party" in the narrative (#52). If a train is involved, list the name of the engineer. Also,

a. If the involved party is a hit-and-run driver, enter as much information as can be verified.

b. For parked vehicles enter only the applicable vehicle information.

c. Noncontact vehicles:

(1) A "noncontact" vehicle and driver should be entered on the front page of Form 555 if the driver committed a traffic violation or other act which caused another party to become involved in a collision, and

(a) The facts are corroborated by a disinterested witness, or

(b) There is sufficient physical evidence at the scene to justify the belief that a "noncontact" vehicle was involved.

(2) When (1) above is applicable, complete the report as a multiple vehicle collision.

(3) When (1) above is *not* applicable, record the alleged "noncontact" driver as a witness on the front page of Form 555 and include his or her statement in the narrative (#52).

(4) When a "noncontact" driver has left the scene, proceed in accordance with the above as the facts and evidence warrant.

21. *Name:* Record the first, middle, and last name of the involved party, and

    a. If the involved party has a driver's license, the name recorded should be exactly as shown on the license. Any difference between a person's true name and the name recorded should be explained in the narrative (#52).

    b. If an involved party is in the armed forces, enter military rank and service or social security number, as applicable, after his last name.

22. *Street Address:* The "party's" current street address, city, state, and phone number are placed here. If any involved party is in the armed forces, enter the branch of service and current military address in this space. Attempt to obtain a business or home phone number where the involved party can be contacted during normal business hours; if a phone number cannot be obtained, enter "none."

23. *Driver's License Number State:* Record the alpha/numeric number as it appears on the driver's license:

    a. If the driver's license is a valid military or government's driver's license, record "Gov" after the license number. (Record this type of driver's license number only if the driver is an employee of the United States Government operating a federally owned or controlled vehicle on official business.)

    b. Enter "EXP" after the license number if the license has expired.

    c. Enter "N.I.P." if driver does not have license in his or her possession.

    d. Enter "None" if driver is unlicensed.

    e. Enter driver's social security number, if available, after an "N.I.P." or "None" entry.

    f. Enter in the narrative section (#52) information on restrictions, endorsements, and the expiration date if the license is expired. Any information as to type of license, driver's classification, etc., considered essential by the reporting officer, should be entered in the narrative section (#52).

    g. Leave this entry blank if not applicable to the involved party.

24. *Birthdate:* Record the numerical month, day, and year that the involved party was born (for example, 6/23/43). (If unable to determine the exact birthdate, enter an estimate of the year of birth followed by a question mark.)

25. *Sex:* Enter "M" for male and "F" for female. If unknown due to collision severity, hit-and-run collision, etc., enter "unk."

26. *Race:* This is an optional entry.

27. *Vehicle Year:* Enter the last two digits of the vehicle model year.

28. *Make:* Enter the manufacturer's trade name or standard abbreviation; for example Oldsmobile: Olds., International®: Int'l. Do not use model names (Pinto®, Monte Carlo®, etc.) unless in conjunction with the manufacturer's name.

29. *License Number and State:* Enter the alpha/numeric vehicle registration number as it appears on the license plate. Compare this number with that on the registration certificate.

    a. Enter "Exp" after the license number if the vehicle license has expired. Enter the standard abbreviations for the name of the state which issued the license plate. If the vehicle is not registered and registration is not required enter "N/A" for not applicable.

    b. If a combination of vehicles is involved in the collision and this space is not adequate for all plate numbers, enter "See narrative" and record the plate numbers in the narrative section (#52).

30. *Owner's Name and Address:* Enter the registered owner's name and address if the driver is not the registered owner. If the driver is the registered owner, check the "Same as Driver" box. If the owner's address is the same as the driver's, check the "Same as Driver" box in this space.

31. *Direction of Travel—On Across (Street or Highway):* Enter the

direction of travel and the official route number or name of the highway, street, alley, etc., upon which the involved party was traveling.

    a. The direction of travel should be entered in accordance with the route destination alignment (general route direction: NS, EW) of the street or highway rather than the true compass direction at the collision location. The direction of travel for vehicles on ramps and connections should be determined by assuming that the route direction of the parent highway is the true direction. If route destination alignment is not known, enter the compass direction. The sketch (#50) and narrative (#52) sections should also show compass direction.

    b. When a collision occurs while a vehicle is making a turn at an intersection and the point of impact is within the intersection, the direction of travel is the direction of the vehicle *prior to the turning movement.* Entries such as "N" or "N to W" are acceptable. When, due to a wide median, etc., there are permanent traffic control devices within an intersection, treat each of the intersecting roadways as a separate intersection; for example, a left turning vehicle subject to a stop sign within an intersection median prior to crossing a second intersecting roadway.

    c. The direction of travel for a vehicle backing or driving into or out of a driveway would be the direction that would be consistent with "across" the street or highway until the vehicle has either completed the forward turning movement or has completed the backing movement and has started forward.

    d. Line out either "on" or "across" as applicable.

  32. ***Speed Limit:*** Enter the *prima facie* speed limit or, when applicable, the maximum speed limit for the vehicle or combination of vehicles upon the highway where the collision occurred.

  33. ***Disposition of Vehicle—On Orders Of:*** Enter the name of the garage or place of storage to which the vehicle was towed, if applicable. If the vehicle was not stored and disposition was directly handled by the driver, this space may be left blank, and an "X" placed in the box titled "By Driver." If the vehicle was removed on orders of other than the driver, insert "owner," or other appropriate designation of persons ordering the disposition in the "On Orders Of" space.

  34. ***Vehicle Damage:*** Determine the extent and location of damage and mark an "X" in the appropriate box.

a. *Minor:* Slight damage such as dents, broken glass, etc.
b. *Moderate:* More than slight, but damage to no more than one fourth of the vehicle; for example, an entire fender, grill, quarter panel, door, hood, trunk deck.
c. *Major:* Damage to more than one fourth of the vehicle, such as the entire side, rear end, etc.
d. *Total:* Apparent damage indicates vehicle is not worth repairing (judgment is based on the age of the vehicle and severity of structural damage).
e. *Location of Damage:* Use "front," "rear," "top," "LS" for left side, "RS" for right side, etc., to indicate location of damage. (Damage and its location and description [#38] is important to the reconstruction of the accident.) Use the narrative section (#52) if additional space is required to describe damage location.

35. *Violation Charged:*
a. This entry applies only to collision-related violations. Other violations should be noted in the narrative (#52). Enter the vehicle code section number and, if applicable, the subsection in the order they are charged on the citation or complaint. Indicate the letter abbreviation of the code violation if other than the vehicle code. Identify city or county ordinance by "City Ord." or "Co. Ord.", when applicable, and enter a brief description of the ordinance in the narrative (#52).
b. If a driver is charged with more than two violations, include the additional charges in the narrative section (#52).
c. If a complaint is to be filed or an owner's responsibility citation is to be issued later, record in the narrative (#52) or "Miscellaneous" (#51) section the information required to complete the citation. (Do not enter information in the "Violation Charged" space unless the citation or complaint is completed prior to distribution of collision report copies.)
d. If a "warning" form is issued to one or more drivers at the scene for minor driver's license, registration, or equipment violations, enter a brief summary of vehicle code sections charged in the narrative section (#52). Such violations should *not* be entered in the "Violation Charged" space.

36. *Party 2:* Use when two parties are involved in the accident, and when more than two parties are involved, use an additional copy or

copies of Form 555, changing #1 and #2 in this section to a number appropriate to the party involved. (See #20, Involved Party Category— Party 1, for guidance as to entries in this section.)

37. ***Property—Description of Damage:*** Enter a description of any property damaged in the collision, other than vehicle(s). Leave this space blank if not applicable.

38. ***Owner's Name and Address:*** When space #37 contains data, enter the name and complete address of the owner or person in charge of the damaged property, other than vehicle(s).

39. ***Notified:*** When data is entered in spaces #37 and #38, mark an "X" in the appropriate box to indicate whether the owner, or person in charge of the damaged property, was notified.

40. ***Witness Only:*** Mark an "X" in this box to indicate an uninjured witness is being described; disregard space calling for data on injured persons and enter only the following: age (#41); sex, "M" or "F" (#42); report's vehicle number if uninjured witness was a passenger in an involved vehicle (#45); full name and address (#46); and telephone number (#47).

41–48. ***Injured Persons:*** The information entered in this section identifies either an injured party or a "witness only." The term "injured" refers to a party who has incurred any injury as a result of the collision.

41. ***Age:*** Enter age of injured party. If age is estimated, indicate by entering age plus a question mark after age.

42. ***Sex:*** Enter "M" for male; "F" for female.

43. ***Extent of Injury:*** Mark an "X" in the box best describing the injured person's condition:

   a. *Fatal Injury:* Dead at the time the collision report is prepared.

   b. *Severe Wound, Distorted Member:* A severe wound is a cut or laceration of the skin from which blood flows freely. It is not an injury that merely oozes blood. A distorted member is an arm, foot, finger, etc., that is not in a normal position, usually due to a fracture or serious sprain.

   c. *Other Visible Injuries:* Bruises are discolored or swollen places where the body has received a blow. Bruises include black eyes and bloody noses. Abrasions are areas of the skin where the surface is roughened or broken by scratches or rubbing. A little blood generally oozes from abrasions. Skinned shins, knuckles, knees, and elbows are abrasions. Swelling is a lump, etc., often combined with a bruise or abrasion.

d. *Complaint of Pain:* This classification is for participants in the collision who say they want to be listed as injured, but do not appear to be so, persons who seem dazed, confused or incoherent (unless such behavior can be attributed to intoxication, extreme age, illness, or mental infirmities), and persons who are limping, but do not have visible injuries. Classify in this group any person who is known to have been unconscious as a result of the collision although it appears he or she has recovered.

44. *Injured Was:* Mark an "X" in a single box classifying the injured person.

45. *In Vehicle Number:* Write in the vehicle number (#1, #2, etc.) in which the injured person was driver or passenger.

46. *Name Address:* Enter the full name and current address of the injured person, or "party 1," "party 2," etc., as appropriate, if the injured person is identified as an involved party in the collision report.

47. Enter a phone number at which the injured party may be contacted during normal business hours. (Entry not required if injured person has been identified as an involved party.)

48. *Taken To:* Enter the name and location of the hospital or doctor to which the injured was transported. If party is to go to his or her own doctor or hospital, enter the applicable information. (On "Late-reported" collisions where injuries are claimed, the reporting officer shall ascertain if medical treatment was received. Enter the name of the hospital or doctor treating the injured party or "Medical Treatment Received."

49. *Injured/Witnesses.* List injured persons first, then "Witnesses Only"

50. *Sketch:* Prepared for each investigation, unless officer did not respond to scene.

51. *Miscellaneous:* Brief notation of data for local needs.

52. *Brief description of event.*

53. *Collision Analysis:* This section "forces" responses from the reporting officer. These responses, within the limits of the information called for, provide for the collection of comprehensive data about the collision. Each subsection requires one entry, except as indicated. Single column subsections relate to the collision and require the reporting officer to mark the relevant element or elements on the first Form 555 used in preparing the collision report. Multicolumn subsections relate to one or more involved "parties," and allow for an "X" to be marked on the "first" Form 555 for up to four (4) involved parties. When five (5) or more

parties are involved in a collision, the numbers 5, 6, 7, 8, etc., should be substituted for the form's 1 through 4 numbering.

In selecting the element or elements of a subsection which best supply the information being sought, the reporting officer should place an "X" in the appropriate space, and when an explanation is necessary, he should footnote the subsection marked and write the explanation in the narrative section (#52).

Entries in this collision analysis section must be in agreement with data reported elsewhere on Form 555.

Traffic Accident/Collision Records System

To attain a reduction in the frequency and severity of traffic collisions it is important that the information exchanged among users be identical in definition and type of data. Collision data, collected statewide in accordance with statewide documentation instructions, will be uniform in type and definition. In California, the statewide Form 555 and its instruction manual provide this basic threshold to a statewide "integrated" traffic records system (see Fig. 19).

The extent to which a statewide system can meet the reporting needs of the data users it must serve has not been fully determined. Time restraints and related cost factors are some of the existing limitations. Sometimes, budgeting limits just do not allow for the purchase or lease, and the operation, of a system that will supply every conceivable need. Unfortunately, less costly and less sophisticated systems obtained to satisfy current minimal requirements are soon outdated and obsolete.

A major requirement of any statewide system is to provide to local, county, and state agencies data which will locate collisions; an *intersection identification index* is one of the more significant phases of the statewide study. It must be, if possible, compatible with the system already used by the planning and other agencies in the cities and counties of the state to allow for transfer of historical data, and it must allow for intersection codes internal to the computer. When a report is retrieved from tape and printed out, the intersection code should reveal the street names of the intersection. This arrangement can be adapted to locate other highway locations between intersections.

The intersection identification index should contain records on all the intersections within the state. Included in this index are such data elements as city and county jurisdiction, X–Y map coordinates, traffic

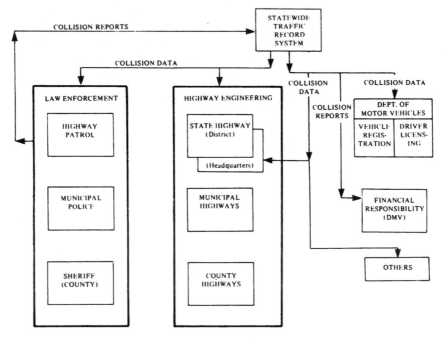

Figure 19. Users of accident reports and collision data in a statewide computerized traffic records system.

volumes and controls, and roadway characteristics. Referrals for each intersection, which identify the next intersection in each direction, facilitate computerized highway "route" or "segment" searches. The distance between adjacent intersections should also be included to enable the computation of mileage accident rates.

The accident history "File" should contain records of reported accidents for a three and one-half-year to four-year period. This file should be updated on a daily basis, and when four (4) or five (5) years of data are accumulated, the earliest year should be purged to an "archives" file.

A selective summary capability for traffic citation and arrest programs should permit storage of citations between selected dates of issuance, by major violation, with the results also sorted for ready access by the locations where the citations were issued.

The accident summaries should permit access and retrieval by any or all of the following:

1. Street on which the accident occurred.
2. Intersecting street (for accidents occurring at intersections).
3. Type of collision (head-on, sideswipe, etc.).

4. Object collided with (fixed object, parked car, pedestrian, etc.).
5. Type of accident (property damage, injury, fatal, etc.).
6. Probable cause of the accident.

An implied objective in any system operating at statewide levels is to develop a system which represents the state of the art with respect to the application of computer technology to the processing of traffic accident data and related information. At the minimum, a statewide system should be able to analyze accidents in ways heretofore impractical using manual procedures, and as a computer-based system is perfected, output from the system should have a capability of being shown in a map-like presentation, to overcome any need for manual procedures to transfer printed output data to maps and other graphic data portrayals.

Computer-produced reports should not only be obtained more quickly, but also should contain more data than manual summaries of the same data, and sufficient data should be provided in computer-produced reports for drawing collision diagrams and making routine analysis of accident causes.

The great promise of statewide "integrated" traffic records systems for police officials and other persons responsible for planning vehicle collision reduction programs is that the storage and retrieval capability of a state's traffic records system will be equal to their needs, and there will be a high "utility" factor in the state system's computer produced reports: retrieval data will be useful in planning vehicle collision reduction programs.

Collision Diagrams

Collision diagrams are based on the belief that a picture is better than many, many words. It is a graphic portrayal of the accident history of a location for the period under study. It is truly amazing how conflict points and a pattern of accidents are revealed by this method of picturing accidents at the site of occurrence.

Any letterhead-size paper can be used. A heading to identify the police unit would be at the top of the sheet. This would be followed by a large intersection sketch containing only the curb lines of the intersection (see Fig. 21).

These diagrams need not be to scale, but they should be neatly

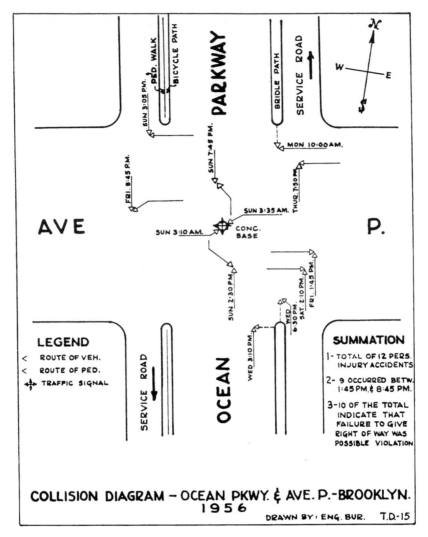

Figure 20. The pattern of accidents in the collision diagram indicates failure to yield the right-of-way as a factor in the accident experience of this intersection.

prepared with attention to detail. Road strips can be handled in a like manner by sketching in road limits instead of the outline of an intersection.

Each accident is indicated on a collision diagram by arrows showing the direction of movement of the traffic units involved. There is no need to indicate the exact spot or location of the accident within the intersection; these diagrams are schematic. The path of each vehicle involved is indicated by a solid-line arrow, and each pedestrian by a dotted-line arrow. The date of the accident is written just above one of the arrows, and its hour of occurrence is placed just below it.

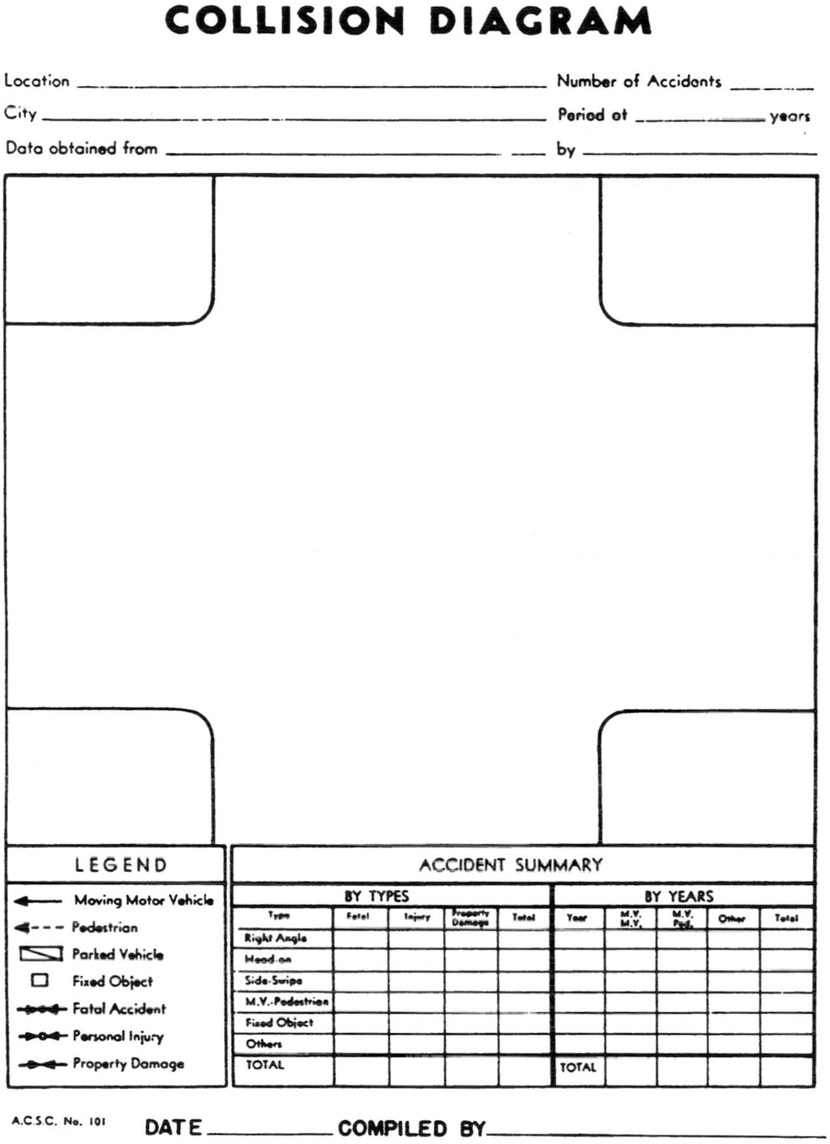

COLLISION DIAGRAM

Location _____ Number of Accidents _____

City _____ Period of _____ years

Data obtained from _____ by _____

LEGEND

◄——— Moving Motor Vehicle

◄- - - Pedestrian

▭ Parked Vehicle

▢ Fixed Object

—●●◄ Fatal Accident

—●�’◄ Personal Injury

—●◄ Property Damage

ACCIDENT SUMMARY

	BY TYPES					BY YEARS				
Type	Fatal	Injury	Property Damage	Total	Year	M.V. M.V.	M.V. Ped.	Other	Total	
Right Angle										
Head-on										
Side-Swipe										
M.V.-Pedestrian										
Fixed Object										
Others										
TOTAL					TOTAL					

A.C.S.C. No. 101   **DATE**_____ **COMPILED BY**_____

Figure 21. Form for preparation of accident/collision diagram.

Brief notations as to fog, snow, or nighttime may be made in the event such data would have a bearing on the analysis of the diagram, but it must be remembered that unnecessary data on these diagrams destroys their effectiveness in presenting an accident pattern. However, if three accidents took place on one snowy night, a notation would be made for the purposes of excluding these accidents in pattern development. The reverse would be true if most accidents happened at night. A notation would then reveal a developing pattern of night accidents calling for improved lighting in addition to any other remedial action. The same rule should be applied to other causal factors concerning an accident.

The pattern development which is revealed by the collision diagram is the key to successful remedial action (see Figs. 20 and 21) and should reveal accidents falling into one or more of the following collision or noncollision patterns:

1. Pedestrian versus vehicle.
2. Right-angle collisions between vehicles entering on intersecting streets.
3. Rear-end collisions of cars moving in the same direction.
4. Head-on left-turn collisions involving vehicles approaching each other from opposing directions.
5. Collisions with parked vehicles.
6. Sideswipe or turning collisions involving vehicles moving in the same direction.
7. Head-on.
8. Collisions with fixed objects.
9. Vehicles running off roadway at curves or restrictions in roadway.

Chapter 15

HIT–AND–RUN ACCIDENTS

Any person operating a motor vehicle or motorcycle in New York State who, knowing that damage has been caused to the property (not including animals) of another or knowing that injury has been caused due to culpability or to accident, leaves without stopping, exhibiting his license, and giving his name, residence, and license number to the person sustaining the damage or injury or to a police officer (or in case a police officer or the person sustaining the damage is not present, then reporting as soon as possible to the nearest police station or judicial officer) is guilty of a misdemeanor.

A police officer may arrest such an individual without a warrant, as a general rule, when in fact the crime has been committed, though not in the officer's presence, and when there is reasonable cause to believe that the person to be apprehended has committed this crime.

Intent is not mentioned as a necessary element of this crime, and ownership of the vehicle involved is immaterial. Injury or damage must result, and the operator fleeing the scene must have knowledge of it. It is immaterial how the accident occurred so long as the operator left the scene without reporting.

Apprehending and prosecuting hit-and-run drivers is necessary for the following reasons:

1. Injury might have been lessened or death prevented if the driver had promptly sought help instead of leaving the accident scene.
2. Streets would not be safe if motorists could flee accident scenes without accepting responsibility. Unless the negligent driver is found, accident victims cannot get compensation for injuries and property damage.
3. Public knowledge that the police usually apprehend and convict hit-and-run drivers deters other drivers who might otherwise be inclined to evade responsibility.

Police units find these leaving-the-scene cases one of their most troublesome categories of crime. They are "heartbreakers" in that the assigned police have difficulty in avoiding personal involvement in attempting to solve a crime without motive and usually without any witnesses. Standard police procedure calls for the issuance of a prompt alarm for the fleeing vehicle, an extensive crime scene search, and assignment of police investigators to the accident-and-crime scene around the time of occurrence, and on days following the accident, in a search for witnesses.

The Hit-and-Run Operator

Hit-and-run drivers have been grouped into three categories based upon possible psychological explanations for their motivation for flight:

1. Apprehensive—panic-driven, fearful driver.
2. Projectionist—projects guilt.
3. The sneak—minor property-damage-only accidents.

The apprehensive driver has a greater sin to hide, either morally or criminally. This individual typically flees the scene for one or more of the following reasons: (1) driving while intoxicated, (2) operating without a license, (3) no insurance, (4) a companion is in the car who is not the driver's mate or who is the mate of another, (5) stolen car, (6) stolen goods in the car, (7) leaving the scene of another accident, (8) fleeing a crime scene, or (9) is wanted for crime.

The projectionist driver tries the case, sitting as judge and jury, finds the other driver at fault, refuses to be a party to the accident, and drives off as the offended person.

The sneak operator is one that crushes a fender and smashes grillwork as daily occupational activities and chalks up the action as the calculated risk shared by all vehicle owners who place their vehicles on the roadway.

Fortunately, the hit-and-run operator does not have the attitudes of a professional criminal, nor is the operator skilled at concealing the damage to the vehicle. They will usually be cooperative when found, and traces of vehicle damage can be easily located, even if recently repaired.

The Alarm

The basic line of investigation in these cases must be along the lines of opportunity: (1) What car was at the scene? and (2) Who operated it? The ideal time of apprehension is while the fugitive car is being operated by the hit-and-run driver. For this reason, time is most important in determining the accident is a hit-and-run case and getting a broadcast on the air.

When investigators find the scene of an accident is a hit-and-run case, their first effort is to obtain from available witnesses a full description of the car involved. This should include odd or unusual details; even noises are sometimes useful. Descriptive items which may prove extremely valuable in locating the vehicle are (1) stickers on windows or windshield, (2) dented fenders, (3) fancy wheel covers, (4) broken radio aerials, (5) distinctive ornaments and fixtures, (6) broken window glass, (7) unusual colors and body styles, and (8) out-of-state license plates.

The above data, together with a description of the occupants and the direction of the vehicle when last seen, should be immediately broadcast in a police radio alarm to all members of the department and to nearby police units.

The alarm alerts police on patrol to look for abandoned vehicles or vehicles in transit with such damage and as described. Particular attention is usually directed along the possible escape routes of the fleeing vehicle.

Garages, parking lots, used car lots, and other places where a vehicle might be stored or taken for repairs shall be promptly checked by police. Generally, if a car is not located within a reasonable time after the accident occurred, it may be assumed that the driver removed it from the streets and placed it in a private garage.

A prearranged list of all public garages and other likely storage places will facilitate the assignment of police cars to conduct preliminary inquiries. Prearranged contacts with garages may result in the immediate reporting of a damaged vehicle.

Officers at the accident scene should also check suspicious persons at the scene or an inquisitive passerby. Sometimes hit-and-run drivers return to the scene from curiosity or to find out how much evidence the police have discovered. In many cases the hit-and-run driver stops from habit, examines the injuries of the victim, stays a few minutes, and then flees. This habit should be kept in mind when questioning witnesses as to information on persons who were at the scene but have driven away.

Police officers should be alert for vehicles reported stolen after the time of the hit-and-run case which answer to the description of the fugitive car. When no description is available, all of these cases of reported thefts should be investigated for possible involvement. It is a common technique of the hit-and-run driver, in attempting to explain vehicle damage and the presence of his or her vehicle at the scene, to flee and then park the vehicle in some out-of-the-way area and report it as being stolen.

The Scene Search

Transfer evidence* is important in hit-and-run investigations. Since the only investigative leads are along the line of opportunity, it is vital to search for evidence at the accident scene which will identify the vehicle and the driver involved. This should not be limited to prime identification which will lead to prompt identification of either the vehicle or operator, but should extend to any evidence which will connect the vehicle and its driver to the scene when the suspect vehicle is located or an apprehension of the fleeing operator is made.

The search for physical evidence at the scene should be thorough. It should be planned so that every part of the area is carefully and methodically searched. A haphazard procedure of searching may frustrate the entire investigation by failing to discover evidence or by destroying or impairing the value of evidence. This is a most important step in the investigation. The scene must be protected and safeguarded, then it must be pointed toward broken headlight glass, door handles, hubcaps, paint marks or scrapings, soil and mud fallen from cars at impact, and any other debris. Objects carried in or on a hit-run vehicle are of value. Damage to fixed objects can also be studied for traces of paint and indication of damage to the vehicle.

Whenever the scene search reveals the nature of the damage to the car or the probable make or model of the car, this information should be immediately added to the alarm and broadcast to all units aiding in the search.

Several police agencies use an artist or a special effects photographer to prepare a graphic illustration of the wanted car on the basis of known information secured in the investigation and probable damage (based on the damage sustained by vehicles involved in previous accidents of a similar nature).

Experienced hit-and-run investigators attempt to identify the original purpose of the hit-and-run driver. What brought the driver into the

---

*Evidence that will connect the suspect with the scene or vice versa.

neighborhood of the accident scene? What brought him or her into this area at the time of the accident, on the day of the week on which the accident happened? This assumption of purposefulness is coupled with the habits of motorists to utilize the same routes to and from work or leisure activity. This is the basis for the concept of returning to the accident scene on stakeout duty in a quest for witnesses; it is also an emerging concept for locating the vehicle involved in a hit-and-run case.

Stakeouts

Investigators should regularly return to the scene looking for new witnesses. The return should be at the same time of day and day of week as of the accident. The neighborhood of the accident, route of travel, and other possible areas should be canvassed thoroughly for new witnesses. Perseverance is the rule, not the exception.

In several New York hit-and-run cases the author was just about ready to quit when patient police work turned up witnesses who did not realize they were the object of our extensive police search as the only eyewitnesses. In one case, all the previous questioning of witnesses led to an attempt to trace a black Chevrolet. A postal employee who had been sick for ten days following the accident was stopped and questioned by police accident investigators who had been assigned to the hit-and-run scene daily around the time of the accident in the quest for witnesses.

"Sure, I know of the accident," he told the inquiring officer, "I saw the green car hit the man." Further questioning revealed he had copied the license number of the car involved but had never turned it in because the driver had stopped and assured him that he would get an ambulance. With this assurance, he stepped into the subway and continued on his way to work. Later investigation showed the driver of the green car had stopped, but took flight when he noticed the absence of other witnesses. When the arrest of the driver of the green car was reported by the papers, the owner of the black Chevrolet came forward and admitted he had also stopped and fled. He explained he had become frightened at being involved and possibly suspected as the criminal, and he had also fled the scene, though he was not involved in the accident.

Another case in which patience was rewarded involved a pedestrian death on a dark, rainy night. The search for witnesses at the accident scene, day after day, led to three operators who had driven over the pedestrian but had not stopped, because they did not believe they had struck him down initially and did not want to get involved in a vehicle homicide case.

In still another case, witnesses placed a car at the scene of a pedestrian hit-and-run accident, but upon locating the suspect driver and car, police investigators found there was little damage to the car. This lack of damage supported the hysterical driver's claim that he had not hit the deceased; the body of the pedestrian involved had been thrown into his path by another car. His story of how the car ahead of his vehicle had carried the body on its hood for about a block and a half before it slowed down sufficiently to disengage the victim and continue on its way was not believed at first, but continued investigation led to a car having damage fitting this story, and upon confrontation the driver confessed.

Transfer Evidence

Science has provided the police with one of their most effective weapons against hit-and-run cases. The scientific analysis of evidence found at an accident scene sometimes identifies the make and model of the wanted car. Comparison analysis of such evidence with that recovered from a suspect's automobile provides data placing the vehicle at the crime scene. Some of the most common types of evidence found in hit-and-run accident investigations are amenable to scientific analysis.

Since the advent of sealed-beam headlights, glass fragments found at accident scenes are not as productive of results as in former years. However, they are still excellent evidence for proving that a suspect car, when located, was at the accident scene. Broken automobile parts, paint, soil, hairs and fibers, bloodstains, and tire marks all lend themselves to the identification of the type and make of car in the first phase of searching for the vehicle, and also to later comparison analysis when the suspect vehicle is located.

When a suspected car is located, it should be impounded for an immediate search for evidence. All exterior parts of the vehicle should be carefully examined. Special attention should be given to all protruding parts where hair or fibers might have been caught. All damaged parts should be noted and inspected for traces of blood or signs of contact with other objects. No foreign material should be discarded from consideration until its source is definitely determined. Evidence of recent damages, repairs, new painting, or wash jobs should be carefully noted.

If damaged parts have been replaced, attempts should be made to obtain the original parts.

The undercarriage of the vehicle should receive special attention. The car should be placed over a mechanic's pit or up on a grease rack for proper search. Spots which appear to have been brushed by an object and all protruding parts should be thoroughly examined for hairs, fibers, and blood spots.

The possibility of developing latent fingerprints to identify the driver of a vehicle must always be attempted. Frequently a suspect denies having driven the vehicle, and it may in fact have been driven by a thief. Fingerprints may tell the story.

All evidence should be properly preserved and compared with evidence found at the scene of the accident so the investigating officer can prove that the suspect's vehicle was at the accident scene and was involved in the accident.

The vehicle is the key to the criminal in these cases. If transfer evidence will connect the vehicle with the accident scene, then police can look to its owner for honest answers in a fact-finding inquiry about the operator.

A common explanation by the owner of the vehicle is that his car may be involved, but he denies driving it at the time and claims he loaned it to a friend of recent acquaintance known to him only as "Joe." *Don't believe it.* In fact, do not believe it until "Joe" is identified and found, and he confesses.

Accountability

Apprehension of a hit-and-run driver is difficult because information can only be secured from victims and witnesses and from physical evidence found at the scene. Informers are of little use in these cases. There is no *modus operandi* to identify the criminal, a suspect usually does not have a record of previous offenses, and this criminal could be any member of the community.

Motive is not a potential line of inquiry in these cases insofar as a desire to kill or injure the victim. Motivation is only for flight from the scene and has no connection with the victim. Therefore the line of inquiry as to who wanted to kill the deceased, which frequently leads to the criminal in homicide cases is useless in these hit-and-run cases.

Car dealers and motor vehicle license authorities can supply the names and addresses of persons recently purchasing a car similar to the wanted vehicle, or having a license number close to the license number of the wanted car, and apprehension can be effected, but a great deal depends on chance.

Legislation has been proposed which requires the licensing of body and fender repair shops in order that regular checks of their shops and records could be made, but no great progress has been made, as it is an unwieldy process to administer effectively.

Hit-and-run investigations should be conducted by accident investigators. When this work is assigned to detective units, it is only human for a detective working on criminal homicides, felonious assaults, kidnappings, and bank robberies to assign a role of lesser importance to hit-and-run cases. Yet in this field of traffic safety the people of a community can be won over to the police side by the quick solution of these cases and prompt apprehension and trial of the offenders. Much of this work can be accomplished by accident investigators working in uniform, but permission should be granted to assigned investigators to work out of uniform when necessary.

Accident investigators are key personnel in getting these investigations started promptly. A prompt alarm and search will result in an apprehension before a car can be hidden and the damage repaired. It will also result in an emotional shock to the fleeing driver which results in an offender's waiving the right to silence and legal counsel and making a prompt and full admission of fleeing the scene and the reasons for such flight.

In New York City, a sergeant of the Accident Investigating Squad short-circuited the normal red tape involved in large city police operations and made an arrest in a few hours. When reports were returned that the suspect operator could not be located at the address given when the car was registered, this sergeant made a one-man search of the neighborhood for someone who knew the suspect. Two blocks away he discovered a sister who promptly divulged her brother's address when it was explained that it would be to his advantage to meet with the police. A prompt apprehension was made before the car could be repaired (in fact, while the radiator was still warm) and an equally prompt admission of guilt was secured.

Another member of the same unit traveled across the city one night with a fragment of a license number and a fragment of radiator grill as his only clues. He had called the motor vehicle bureau and secured about ten names and addresses of possible suspects from the license number fragment. He visited each of the persons listed, asked to look at their cars, and met resistance on the last visit—but it was only resistance to arrest. The sergeant had matched the radiator grill fragment with a car parked in front of the suspect's home and registered in the suspect's name. Confronted with this evidence, the hit-and-run driver apologized for his resistance and admitted that he had been drinking and driving and was afraid of being arrested for drunken driving.

The assignment of accountability for hit-and-run investigations to persons trained in accident investigation is an excellent specialization joining the field of traffic and criminal investigation.

Possible Murder

Infrequently, a pedestrian, walking or jogging on a sidewalk or the side of a road, is struck by a fast-moving vehicle. Dead on arrival at the local hospital before police arrived, the case goes into the hit-and-run routine without results.

The local Homicide Squad should be notified whenever there is the slightest evidence of murder and asked to run a regular homicide check on who might "profit from or want the victim dead."*

In the meantime, the traffic H & R investigator concentrates on finding the damaged car and witnesses.

---

*Paul B. Weston, and Kenneth M. Wells, *Criminal Investigation—Basic Perspectives,* 5th ed. (Englewood Cliffs, NJ, Prentice-Hall, 1990), pp. 273–293.

Chapter 16

TRAFFIC ENGINEERING

Traffic engineering begins with the street and highway system of a community, moves to planning and designing improvements, and necessarily includes finding funds for major physical changes in the streets and highways of a locality. In America, most traffic engineers have a maestro's ability to accommodate existing traffic volume and density to the capacity of their roadways within the limitations of public funding.

Normally, no attempt is made to design or operate highways so as to eliminate congestion altogether. The cost of reducing congestion usually exceed the benefits of faster travel. A highway large enough to allow free-flowing traffic during the A.M. and P.M. peak periods is seldom optimal, because building such capacity is very expensive and benefits only a small group of motorists.*

Types of Roadways

The function of *local streets* is to provide access from a collecting street to abutting land and properties. The characteristics of local streets are (1) low speeds, (2) low volume, (3) provide access to abutting lands, (4) provide for turning moves to give access to local establishments, and (5) curb parking.

Collecting streets provide access from a local street to a major arterial system. Such streets must provide access to business establishments and local residences while at the same time providing for through traffic movement and more efficient operation than local streets. While speeds are as low as local streets, a collecting street handles a greater volume of traffic, though providing only limited curb parking.

Major arterial streets provide for the through movement of large

---

*John R. Meyer & Jose A. Gomez-Ibanez, *Autos Transit and Cities* (Cambridge, MA, Harvard University Press, 1981), p. 187.

volumes of traffic. While streets in this category may serve abutting property, the primary purpose of these roadways is to provide uninterrupted movement of a high volume of through traffic. They are characterized by access control and no parking.

Expressways or thruways provide for the through movement of large volumes of traffic between major traffic generating areas. Characterized by the uninterrupted flow of large volumes of traffic at high speed over long distances between major traffic generating areas or through a city or other area of congestion, these roadways not only have limited access and no parking, but also have deceleration and acceleration lanes as well as adequate shoulders or turnouts for the emergency parking of disabled vehicles.

In linking the Interstate Highway System with numbered state and local highways, traffic engineers established business, bypass, alternate, and temporary routes.

Business route is a route within the limits of a municipality which provides motorists an opportunity to pass through the business section. Business routes connect with the regular numbered route at the opposite side of the business section or city limits.

Bypass route is a "relief" route established for motorists wishing to entirely bypass a city or congested area. Bypass routes join in with the regular numbered route beyond the city or congested area. Signs designating this route may be lettered "Bypass" or "Relief Route."

Alternate route is a route that branches off from the regular numbered route, passes through certain cities and towns, and then connects again with the regular numbered route. This is a designation used for old or new routes which cannot conveniently be integrated with the regular numbered route.

Temporary route is a detour on which signs numbering the route and carrying the legend "Temporary Route" designate a road only until the permanently established route is completed and opened to traffic.

Normal police terminology is essentially the same as the traffic engineer's in describing land usage and occupancies. Business, residential, park, and farm areas all have a uniform meaning, whether on the reports of a traffic engineer or a police traffic control officer.

Both individuals also utilize the terms *downtown area* to denote that portion of a city where there are normally large numbers of pedestrians and a heavy demand for parking space, and *outlying area* to describe a residential or sparsely settled area, regardless of occupancies, characterized by few pedestrians and little parking demand, and usually located on the fringe of a municipality.

Capacity

In 1950 the Bureau of Public Roads of the U.S. Department of Commerce issued the *Highway Capacity Manual,* establishing uniform definitions. The great majority of these terms were based on current usage or are definitions as spelled out by authoritative organizations; others represent a combination of definitions appearing in previously published material. Police use of these definitions will convey definite meaning to others in the traffic control field and thus minimize the likelihood of misinterpretation.

Capacity, without modification, is a generic expression pertaining to the ability of a roadway to accommodate traffic. Many elements of street and highway design, vehicle and driver performance characteristics, and traffic control measures directly influencing the movement of vehicles and pedestrians are all summed up in the one word.

Capacity criteria must also include the speed of vehicles, spacing between vehicles, the relative interference between vehicles, as well as the number of vehicles that can pass a point on a roadway in a specified period of time.

Roadway capacity depends primarily upon (1) composition of traffic, (2) alignment of the roadway, (3) number and width of lanes, and (4) speeds of vehicles using the roadway. These prevailing conditions are divided into two groups: (1) prevailing roadway conditions and (2) prevailing traffic conditions.

Prevailing Roadway Conditions. These conditions are determined by the physical characteristics of the roadway, and do not change unless some construction or reconstruction work is performed. Poor planning and design of a highway may result in a roadway whose prevailing roadway conditions make it difficult to move traffic without accidents when the roadway is operated well within the limits of planned capacity.

Prevailing Traffic Conditions. Conditions of traffic are dependent upon the vehicles and pedestrians using the roadway. These conditions may change during various seasons of the year, periods of the day, and in some locations, from hour to hour. Prevailing traffic conditions are also affected by holidays, parades, sporting events, construction, and other traffic generators or hindrances. Possibly the worst prevailing traffic conditions exist just before and immediately following major three-day holidays. Police can expect most streets and highways leading out of a city to exceed capacity from 3:00 PM TO 8:00 PM on Friday and can also expect equal traffic conditions on the return trip from 3:00 PM to 10:00 PM on Monday.

There are three levels of roadway capacity. It is important that police officers use the terminology developed to uniformly identify the various levels of roadway capacity. These terms are (1) *basic capacity,* (2) *possible capacity,* and (3) *practical capacity.*

Basic Capacity. This is the term used for the maximum number of vehicles that can pass on a given lane or roadway during one hour under the most nearly ideal roadway and traffic conditions which can possibly be attained. Actually, this is a theoretical measure, as it is most difficult to secure ideal conditions when roadways are subject to maximum use.

Possible Capacity. This refers to the maximum number of vehicles that can pass a given point on a lane or roadway during one hour under the prevailing roadway and traffic conditions. This is a positive measure or quantity. It cites a traffic volume that cannot be exceeded without changing one or more of the prevailing conditions.

Practical Capacity. This means the maximum number of vehicles that can pass a given point on a roadway or in a designated lane during one hour without the traffic density being so great as to cause unreasonable delay, hazard, or restriction to a driver's freedom to maneuver under the prevailing roadway and traffic conditions.

Practical capacity is also a theoretical measure that has marked subjectivity as to the evaluation of the point at which a driver's freedom to maneuver is unduly delayed, restricted, or made hazardous. Though formulae have been developed for determining the traffic volumes at which a driver's freedom of movement is curtailed by his own speed and other vehicles on the highway, their application requires a great deal of individual judgment.

Satisfactory Capacity. There is a great range between possible and practical capacities. Generally, local traffic engineers develop the intermediate term *satisfactory capacity.* This term denotes the level of operating conditions acceptable as satisfactory by the majority of local motorists.

The most important factors that may reduce practical capacity are the following:

1. Lanes less than twelve feet wide have a lower capacity.

2. Retaining walls, bridge abutments, parked cars, etc., all reduce the effective width of a traffic lane, cause lane-straddling, and result in lower capacity.
3. Lack of adequate shoulders also reduces the effective width of a traffic lane by causing vehicles to shy away from the edge of the pavement and travel toward the center of the roadway. The greatest reduction in capacity occurs when the width of the shoulders of a road will not permit the parking of a disabled vehicle out of the traffic lane.
4. Commercial vehicles occupy a greater road space and influence other traffic more than other passenger cars. They are slow moving, especially on grades, and are slower to close gaps.
5. When drivers are restricted in their freedom of movement by restricted sight distances, the capacity of the road will be lowered. Sight distances of from 1500 to 2000 feet are necessary on two- and three-lane rural highways.
6. Controlled intersections impair highway capacity by depriving the traffic stream of a portion of the time during which it would otherwise be on the move.

Time Patterns

Prevailing traffic conditions are divided into five time patterns (cyclical variation in traffic volumes) on a basis of traffic volumes at different periods of the day. These easy reference periods are as follows:

AM Peak..7:00 to 9:30 AM
Daytime Off-peak...9:30 AM to 4:30 PM
PM Peak ....4:30 to 7:30 PM
Evening Off-peak ....7:30 PM to 12:30 AM
Early Morning Off-peak ....12:30 to 7:00 AM

The characteristics of these time patterns differ, but all are quite stable. The prevailing traffic conditions of both the morning and the afternoon peak periods are very close. The afternoon peak period shows more cars in movement in a slightly shorter time, with commercial areas clearing up shortly after 6:00 PM, though parkway and major highway capacities hold up through 7:00 PM.

Next in demands upon the capacity of the streets and highways are the evening off-peak hours. This is followed by the daytime off-peak, though it must be pointed out that shopping and commercial centers make optimum capacity demands on their local and collecting streets during this period.

The early morning off-peak period picks up after the theater crowd has diminished, and though light in the actual number of cars in motion, this period has a safety problem because vehicles are moving at higher speeds than during any other daily period. Fatal accidents are frequent, and this time period is characterized by a high percentage of "lost control" accidents involving contact with opposing traffic, trees, light poles, and other fixed objects by intoxicated drivers.

Volume

Volume has been defined as the number of vehicles moving in a specified direction or directions on a given lane or roadway which pass a given point during a specified period of time (hourly, daily, etc.).

Determination of volume is basic to the evaluation of any traffic movement. Volume counts show the relative importance of any street or highway by furnishing a basic scale. The police traffic control officer must secure volume data to end up with a knowledge of traffic volume characteristics throughout his area of jurisdiction so that he may understand the time and route distributions for various areas.

Volume counting may be by hand, with manually operated counters or with automatic counters. A single officer with a supply of pencils, forms, a clipboard, and a watch may suffice for one problem. Several automatic counters using pneumatic action on air tubes over which traffic passes may be necessary to secure information for remedial action in another instance. Directional automatic counters offer a new methodology.

Counting periods should be kept as short as possible to avoid expensive full-count procedures. The purpose of the study, the normal rate of fluctuation in the traffic stream, and the basic characteristics of the roadway will be the controlling factors in determining the length of time period that will be necessary. Pedestrian volume is measurable in a like manner and can be integrated with vehicle volumes.

Hourly volumes are practical working units in both design and operation of roadways. For any given road there is one hour during each year when traffic volume is at its peak. This is known as the *maximum hour*. Designing roads to meet maximum hour demands is not practical; therefore traffic engineers select a lesser capacity represented by the thirtieth highest annual hourly volume (the hourly volume on a given roadway exceeded by only twenty-nine hourly volumes in a designated year) as a practical base of highway design.

The Traffic Lane

A strip of roadway intended to accommodate a single file of moving vehicles is a traffic lane. Lanes may be as narrow as nine feet on low-speed streets, but eleven or twelve feet—or more—is required on high-speed highways.

The distribution of vehicles into lanes is vital to the capacity of any given roadway. The basic factor in this distribution is the geometrical design of the roadway, but the condition of the road, the width and number of lanes, parking, accidents, and disabled cars all influence traffic streams and their distribution into lanes.

Single lane routes only permit one-way direction of flow at a time and limit the speed of individual units to that of the car ahead, since they do not permit overtaking and passing. The two-lane route in one-way operation permits overtaking and passing, while the two-lane route in two-way operation curtails such overtaking and passing and creates platoons of vehicles, each led by a slow moving vehicle.

On three-lane roadways in two-lane operation, in which the center lane is to be used for overtaking and passing, it has been found that the center lane will be preempted during peak volume periods for the exclusive movement of traffic in the major flow direction. However, the police traffic control officer may reduce this conflict by utilizing reversible lane procedures to legitimize this unbalanced flow.

Vehicle distribution in a two-lane, one-way traffic stream has been found to equalize in both lanes when the total hourly volume of both lanes reaches about 1700 vehicles. Below this volume the percentage of vehicles in the right-hand lane will be larger than that in the left-hand lane.

Four-lane, two-way roadways distribute the stream generally in accordance with existing origin and destination demands; top volume is usually unbalanced with two vehicles moving in one direction for each vehicle moving in the other direction.

Multilane one-way roadways having three or more lanes reveal characteristics which are unusual; both outside lanes carry the highest percentage of vehicles at low volumes, with the center lane being utilized only as volume increases and faster moving vehicles move into the center lane.

The Traffic Stream

The operators of motor vehicles are statistical oddballs; they act in such a manner that it is difficult to average their reactions while part of the traffic stream. Each driver is a separate and distinct unit, having only limited coherence to other units on the street or highway.

The longitudinal position of vehicles in the traffic stream is the single factor which gives a driver either a sense of safety with some freedom of movement or a sense of hazard and congestion with no freedom to maneuver. As the traffic volume increases, each driver is affected more and more by his fellow motorists, with the high-speed driver feeling this restriction more than the driver operating at normal speeds.

In seeking out the causes of an accident, or in trying to develop a pattern of occurrence at accident prone locations, the police traffic safety officer is better prepared to investigate when he has an understanding of the factors which affect the traffic stream performance of drivers generally. Factors which influence a driver are as follows:

1. General arrangement, width, and other design characteristics of roadway.
2. Surface condition.
3. Lanes—width, number, marked or otherwise separated.
4. Sight distances.
5. Gradients—particularly where the crest of a hill shortens sight distance.
6. Intersections—type and number along route.
7. Roadway appurtenances.
8. General aspect or appearance of the route being travelled.
9. Parking.
10. Traffic control devices.
11. Traffic regulations.
12. Pedestrians.
13. Weather, lighting, and other environmental conditions.[11]
14. Length of trip.
15. Condition of the car.
16. Traffic density.

The extent to which any one driver will be influenced by any of these factors depends in a large degree on his own individual idiosyncracies, driving ability, and experience. In evaluating accident causation to determine the circumstances surrounding an accident, the alert investigator will find the above list useful. In going a little beyond the collision diagram of an accident-prone intersection, this list of factors will also provide background information as to why an accident pattern has developed.

Density

This is a term for the conflict between operators of vehicles pushed closer and closer together by the volume of the traffic stream. Density has been described as the number of vehicles occupying a unit length of the moving lanes of a roadway at a given instant. *Critical density* occurs when the volume of a highway is at its possible capacity and all vehicles are moving at or about the optimum speed (average speed at which traffic must move when the volume is at a maximum on a given roadway).

Accidents occurring during periods of critical density are usually of the "pile-up" type. In New York's parkway system as many as twenty-three cars have been involved in one accident during a period of high critical density on the Gowanus Parkway. Another hazard during a critical density period on multilane expressways with three or more lanes is the plight of the motorist who is unfortunate enough to stall his car in one of the center lanes. He is usually isolated until a police officer rescues him or until the density lessens and sufficient gaps develop for the motorist to reach a shoulder of the road to seek help.

Gaps

These unoccupied road spaces ahead of each vehicle determine the distribution of vehicles in any one-way traffic stream. Gaps are measured from head to head of successive vehicles. The size of a gap is usually stated in feet (when stated in units of time it is termed a "headway"). Each gap includes its own vehicle length; thus one-half mile of roadway includes gaps totaling one-half mile in length.

Variations of gap length in a traffic stream may range from a few feet in bumper-to-bumper traffic to relatively great distances during the early morning time period. Gap length is related to the overall density at the time of traffic stream observation. At lower speeds gaps have a tendency to be fairly uniform, but as the speed of the traffic stream increases, so does the variation in gap length.

Merging Traffic

Merging traffic cannot be accomplished until an adequate gap occurs in the lane into which the merging driver wishes to move. An ideal merging maneuver should be carried out without retarding the rear vehicle concerned. While most delays are borne by the merging vehicles, there is also delay to vehicles in the lanes of traffic into which the merging takes place.

When the merging vehicle is stationary (as occurs when entering a parkway after a required full stop) or moving slowly, average drivers require larger gaps for merging; but when the merging vehicle's speed approaches that of the rear vehicle, relatively short gaps are accepted for merging by most drivers. Acceleration and deceleration lanes on modern highways provide space for merging vehicles to adjust speeds for the purpose of entering or leaving a fast moving traffic stream.

All merging maneuvering has a definite conflict area. This area begins at a safe distance back of the collision area and extends to a point beyond where the merging vehicle has gained approximately normal speed (see Fig. 22). The collision area extends from the point of entry of the merging vehicle to the far end of the area of conflict.

Diverging Traffic

The diverging vehicle develops an area of conflict in the lane from which it departs, and when this maneuver is made from the wrong lane of a multilane roadway, the inherent hazard of leaving a highway is increased, and the conflict area extends from the point of initial movement to the point where the diverging vehicle clears the path of the rear vehicle.

Even when made from the correct lane this diverging maneuver creates some conflict unless traffic volume is very low, as the diverging vehicle must slow up in order to make a turn. This creates the possibility of a rear-end collision so long as the turning vehicle remains in its original lane of travel.

The Crossing Maneuver

No greater conflict exists in the time-space relationship of vehicles to each other than in this maneuver. The conflict area extends some dis-

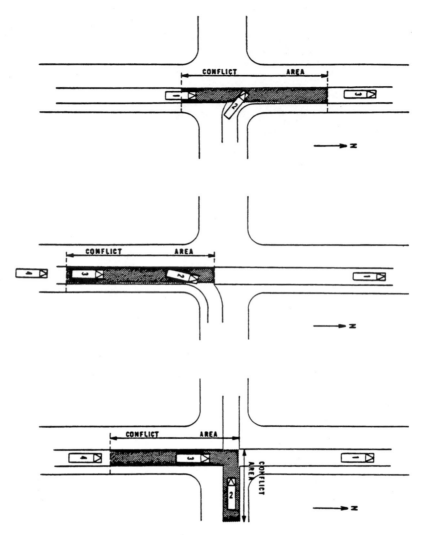

Figure 22. Conflict areas at an intersection during basic traffic movements: *Top:* merging. *Center:* diverging. *Bottom:* crossing.

tance from the intersection or crossing and naturally extends through the collision area (see Fig. 22). Limited observation, the speeds of the vehicles concerned, the type of vehicle crossing contemplated (right-angle, oblique, or opposed left-turn), and the volume of vehicles in each flow determine relative degrees of interference to crossing traffic. Safety at the intersection may require some form of traffic control. Control lessens the capacity of the entering traffic streams, but reduces conflict in the interests of safety.

Intersections

Safety and capacity must be integrated for the satisfactory operation of an intersection; both are of immediate importance. Safety may require stops not called for by actual conflict arising from basic maneuvers. Intersections are heavy with conflict areas in which collisions may occur; for this reason they are of particular interest to persons engaged in accident reduction.

The normal right-angle intersection of two two-way streams of traffic develops thirty-two conflict points, of which half are of the collision-potential crossing type.

The number of potential conflicts per hour is dependent upon vehicle volume in each flow of traffic. Normally about 10 percent of the volume in each flow of traffic turns left, 10 percent turns right, and the remaining 80 percent continues ahead. When each entering stream carries 200 vehicles per hour, approximately 1200 potential conflicts are created in each hour.

Signalization of an intersection reduces capacity as much as 25 percent and possibly more. Generally, the factors that influence basic capacity at intersections are (1) turning movements, (2) commercial vehicles, (3) pedestrian interference, and (4) weather and other environmental conditions.

Practical capacity of any intersection approach is the maximum volume that can enter the intersection from that approach during one hour, with most of the drivers being able to clear the intersection without waiting for more than one complete signal cycle.

One-way Streets

Extensive one-way street or avenue application is within the province of the traffic engineer. The far reaching advantages of one-way streets to the community as a whole in increasing capacity and reducing conflict more than offset the often theoretical disadvantages to individuals and firms in the affected area resulting from loss of traffic in one direction.

There are three types of one-way streets:

Class I: One-way direction at all times.

Class II: One-way direction reversed during certain hours of the day.

Class III: One-way direction during peak periods, reversed to meet commuter traffic demands, and returned to normal two-way operation during off-peak periods.

Collision Patterns

Patterns will develop from collisions; there may be more than one pattern, but at least one will usually develop. The police traffic officer must seek to determine reasons for the occurrence of accidents: a conflict of some kind.

In the field of traffic safety this phase of accident reduction can be compared to scientific criminal investigation. First a *trace* is found; this leads to a *clue* of sorts, and further study will usually resolve the problem. In the detection of crime, the police investigator makes inquiries along the lines of opportunity and motive; in detecting accident patterns, the traffic analyst makes inquiries in the fields of capacity and conflict.

Traffic Control Devices

A traffic control device is any sign, signal, marking, or device used to regulate, warn, or guide traffic. There are three types of these devices: (1) regulatory (separate and sort traffic flow), (2) guiding or informational, and (3) warning—potentially dangerous road and/or traffic conditions.

These devices are the "tools" of the traffic engineer. How and where to use them depends upon the traffic stream's flow and density, developing patterns of movement, and conflict areas.

Supplementing traffic control devices and their placement are traffic engineering studies. These are field checks of physical conditions in and about the roadways and voluntary compliance with stop signs, speed limits, and traffic signals by motorists and pedestrians.

Traffic engineers, working down from their street and highway systems' high accident frequency locations, develop a great understanding of accident patterns and the relationships between traffic flow and traffic control devices.

Traffic Control System in Action

Traffic engineering represents all the men and women functioning under the umbrella of "street and highway engineers" in the traffic control system, and they make a major contribution to the work of other units in the system. Distant from automakers and legislators, they work with cars as they appear in their traffic flow and respect the law as it is written. However, they have a here-and-now relationship with police organizations, the DMV, and EMS.

The goal of a significant safer driving and walking experience may be distant in the time frame of reality, but there are men and women reaching out for it—and daily getting closer.

SELECTED BIBLIOGRAPHY

Ferry, Ted S.: *Modern Accident Investigation and Analysis.* New York, John Wiley, 1988.

Meyer, John, R.; and Gomez-Ibanez, Jose A.: *Autos Transit and Cities.* Cambridge, Harvard University Press, 1981.

Morrison, Kevin M.: *Speed Measurement in Traffic Law Enforcement—From Radar To Laser.* Jacksonville, University of North Florida, 1995.

Rivers, R. W.: *Traffic Accident Field Measurements and Scale Diagrams Manual.* Springfield, Thomas, 1983.

Ross, Gerald; and Kay, Michael: *Toppling the Pyramids—Redefining the Way Companies Are Run.* New York, Times, 1994.

Schwartz, John I.; *Police Roadblock Operations.* Springfield, Thomas, 1962.

Wambaugh, Joseph: *The Onion Field.* New York, Dell, 1983.

Weston, Paul B.: *Combat Shooting for Police.* Springfield, Thomas, 1960.

Periodicals:

FBI Law Enforcement Bulletin
Police Chief
Police Research Bulletin
Traffic Safety

GLOSSARY

Appearance: Response to traffic citation, paying stipulated fine in person or by mail or appearing in court at time and date required.

BAC: Blood alcohol concentration.

Capacity: Ability of a road to accommodate traffic.

Deal: A corrupt opportunity to avoid DUI conviction by plea negotiations (charge is reduced to reckless driving and defendant pleads guilty).

DMV: Department of Motor Vehicles.

DUI: Driving under influence (alcohol/drugs).

EMS: Emergency medical services.

Fix: A corrupt opportunity to avoid a DUI conviction at trial.

Hallucinogenic: Mind-bending drug/substance, distorts reality.

Implied Consent: Highway drivers deemed to have given consent to chemical testing of blood, breath, or urine to determine BAC, if lawfully arrested for DUI.

Jaywalking: Pedstrian crossing street dangerously despite traffic flow.

Misdemeanor murder: Murder is a felony, a capital offense; a vehicle homicide/manslaughter charge limits a sentence upon conviction to ten (or less) years—no life term, death sentence.

Near side: Section of intersection first entered by vehicle.

No-fix: Citation control by court to prevent tampering or other corrupt action (traces citation from officer serving it to final disposition in court).

Per Se: By itself.

Points: Scorekeeping for driver control by courts and DMV.

Prima facie: At first view; uncontradicted.

Reasonable and prudent person: A just, fair, sensible person with ordinary wisdom, carefulness and sound judgment. (Used in situations of care versus negligence.)

Routine stop: Traffic stops without problems have a numbing impact on officers. No-problem stops tranquilize, officers are calm and uninfluenced by cues/signs of fast-breaking violence. Officer survival demands recognition that traffic stops are *never* routine.

Scofflaw: Motorist indicating contempt for laws, police, and courts by ignoring parking "tickets", and failing to appear in court in response to citations. (Scofflaws often owe thousands of dollars in unpaid fines; police use outstanding warrants to apprehend; scofflaws often driving while license suspended or revoked.)

Sobriety: Sober, not drunk or intoxicated.

State's rights: Rights of states as opposed to federal government.

Ms. Erin Fraley compiled these terms, words, and phrases common to police traffic control.

Spike stick: Device to puncture tires of vehicle being pursued by police or failing to stop at roadblock.

Stakeout: Prompt assignment of police to scene of hit and run accident in days/weeks after accident, in time frame centered on time of accident, to seek witnesses by interviewing passing motorists, pedestrians, and others.

Transfer evidence: Physical evidence (things, traces) found at scene of hit and run accident and likely to link suspect vehicle with scene.

Volume: Total number of vehicles moving in a specified direction on a highway past a given point in a time frame of hours or daily.

Wave-off: Failing to make an arrest for DUI when an arrest was warranted. (U.S. Navy term warning pilots against carrier landing.)

INDEX